THE HIMALAYAS

THE HIMALAYAS

BOB GIBBONS

PAUL DAVIES

B.T. Batsford Ltd

ISBN 0 7134 5943 3

Typeset by Servis Filmsetting Ltd, Manchester
and printed and bound in Great Britain by
Butler and Tanner, Frome, Somerset
for the publishers B.T. Batsford Ltd
4 Fitzhardinge Street, London W1H 0AH

Acknowledgements
All black and white photographs are by Bob
Gibbons, except: Bob Ashford 16, 17, 21, 26, 27,
39, 50, 53, 54, 58, 60, 64; Peter Wilson 22, 23 and
42; Pat Robinson 31.
Colour photographs: Bob Gibbons 1–3; John
Pilkington 4, 5; Michael Green 6–10.

Frontispiece
The upper Langtang valley, Nepal, after a light
overnight snowfall in late February.

Contents

List of Black and White Illustrations

List of Colour Plates

(between pages 64 and 65)

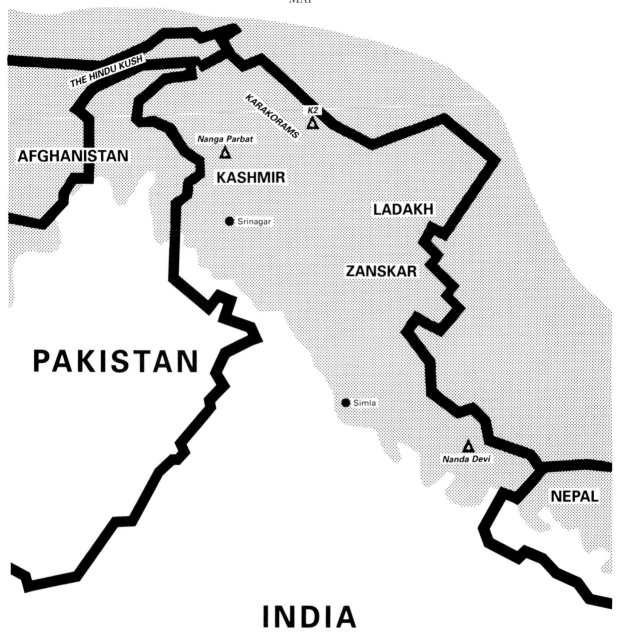

THE HIMALAYAS

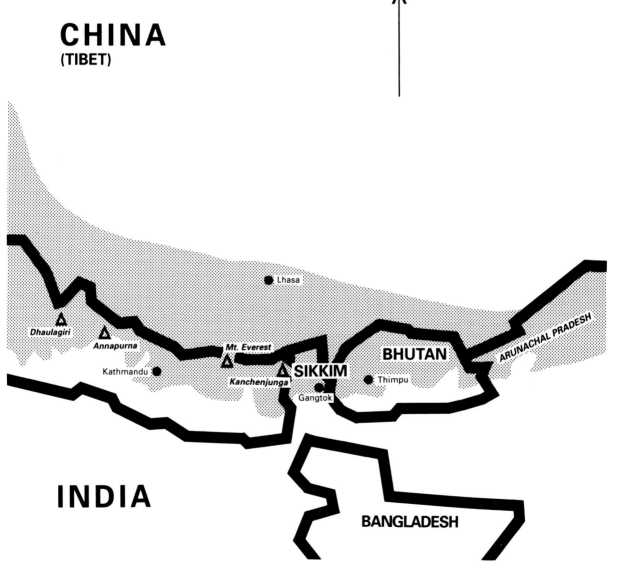

Land over 1500m within the Himalayas

100 miles

160 kms

N

CHINA
(TIBET)

Lhasa

Dhaulagiri

Annapurna

Mt. Everest

Kathmandu

Kanchenjunga

SIKKIM

Gangtok

Thimpu

BHUTAN

ARUNACHAL PRADESH

INDIA

BANGLADESH

CHAPTER ONE

Introduction

The Himalayas are, in almost every way, superlative. They are easily the highest mountain range on Earth, with just about all of the highest mountains in them; they form one of the greatest physical and cultural barriers, and they are stupendously beautiful, still relatively unspoilt, and full of fascinating human and natural life. In many cases, the way of life has remained almost totally unchanged by modern inventions, and it is like going back hundreds, or even thousands, of years.

Until quite recently, the Himalayas were, as far as the Western world was concerned, the domain of a privileged or determined few. The British in India, of course, visited the Himalayas, and established hill stations in the early nineteenth century—like Simla, Srinagar and Darjeeling—which were very popular, though a great part of the Himalayas was either closed to, or unvisited by the British. It was really only with the opening up of Nepal—the country that contains most of the best-known Himalayan peaks—in the 1950s that the Himalayas started to become popular as somewhere to go on holiday, and now almost everywhere is open to visitors, though not necessarily easily accessible or frequently visited. It would be easy to think, from reading newspaper reports and brochures, that just about everywhere in the Himalayas is easily reached and suffering from hordes of littering visitors, but this could hardly be further from the truth. There *are* a few trails that have become abused in this way, but they are a tiny proportion of the vast area of land open to the resourceful visitor.

It is Nepal that still leads the current opportunities for tourism, and they are infinitely more prepared for the visitor, especially those who wish to go walking, than any other part of the mountain range. But India, in particular, is encouraging more visitors to its Himalayan sections, and making it somewhat easier for them, whilst Sikkim (now part of India), Bhutan, Tibet and Pakistan are all gradually becoming more accessible, though numbers are often limited. The only exception to this trend is Afghanistan, where it used to be possible—admittedly, with a lot of effort cutting through bureaucratic resistance—to visit the high mountains in the north-east of the country; few people would consider this practical at present.

This book attempts to explain the background to the incredible Himalayas—why they are there at all, what they are like, who lives there and how they got there, and what the natural life consists of. It then goes on to describe some of the opportunities that the Himalayas have to offer, in a more practical way. A few people simply fly in, have a quick look and take a few pictures, gasp for breath, then fly out again, as part of an 'Asian tour'. Most people, though, stay a little longer, and many are tempted to venture into the roadless hills, perhaps for the all-round experience of trekking in wild and beautiful country, perhaps to see some of the birds or flowers for which the Himalayas are

renowned, or perhaps to see so many different races of people, living in simple harmony with their surroundings, at first hand. Others come to take photographs, climb, ski or raft, and all these possibilities are discussed in greater detail.

The influx of visitors, however, and the changing patterns of life—partly in response to the visitors—are causing many environmental problems, and in the final chapter we look at some of the ways in which the governments are

1. The attractive Gurung village of Birethanti, below Annapurna, Nepal.

tackling these problems, and what visitors themselves should do about them. Any visitor to the Himalayas, for whatever reason, should take a small part of the responsibility for seeing that they never become spoilt, as so many places in the world have been.

CHAPTER TWO

The Physical Nature of the Himalayas

First, we should begin by defining what is meant by the Himalayas. In fact, this is not as easy as it sounds, for the Himalayas are part of one of the most massive and complex mountain systems in the world, and they do not end neatly by petering out at each end. The mountain ranges that fan out from the ends of the Himalayas—many of them of considerable height themselves—have their own names, but are also often referred to as 'Himalayas' at the same time. Nigel Nicolson, in his book on the Himalayas (see Bibliography), illustrates the point by reference to a telephone conversation, requesting an entry permit, with the Afghan Embassy. When asked why he wished to visit Afghanistan, he replied that he was writing a book on the Himalayas: 'We have no Himalayas in Afghanistan,' replied the embassy official! This is true, in a sense, for the Afghan mountains are mainly classed within the Hindu Kush, though it is quite obvious from a glance at a relief map that the Afghan mountains are part of the Himalayas—if not in name.

For the purpose of this book, a slightly variable definition has been adopted. As far as the practical aspects go, such as trekking, I have taken the core area of the Himalayas, from Pakistan in the west to Bhutan in the east, as being the relevant part. However, for the purposes of describing how the Himalayas formed, how their people colonized them, how they have acted as a barrier, and other general features, I have strayed outside this area to Afghanistan in the west and China in the east.

To the south, the definition of the Himalayas is fairly straightforward, since they descend quite quickly through a series of so-called 'foothills'—themselves much higher than the mountains of many countries—down to the Indian subcontinent's plains at a uniformly low altitude. To the north, though, the relief is much more complex, and the Tibetan plateau stretches away for ever at an average height of about 4500 m (14,800 ft), with many much higher peaks. For practical purposes, though, the Himalayas end quickly enough to the north, since they drop away to this level quite sharply, and at present there is virtually no normal access or activity in Tibet or the northern Himalayas.

There is no doubt, however, about one thing: the Himalayas are undoubtedly the highest mountain range on Earth. All of the world's highest mountains lie within the broader definition of the Himalayas, and there are over 30 peaks with an altitude greater than 7600 m (or 16 peaks with a height greater than 26,000 ft, if you are non-metric). Just for comparison, the highest peaks in some other continents are Mont Blanc in Europe (4807 m; 15,781 ft—barely half the height of Everest!); Kilimanjaro in Africa (5890 m; 19,340 ft); Mount McKinley in North America (6190 m; 20,320 ft); and even the highest peak in the Andes, Aconcagua in Argentina—often thought of as comparable to the Himalayas in height—is only 6959 m (22,834 ft). This is lower than many unnamed Himalayan peaks, let alone all the higher, named ones!

2. Glacial lake on the Tibetan border, west of Kala Pattar.

The Highest Himalayan Peaks

		metres	feet
Everest (Sagarmatha)	Nepal	8848	29,028
K2 (Godwin Austen)	Pakistan	8611	28,250
Kanchenjunga	Nepal/Sikkim	8598	28,209
Makalu	Nepal	8481	27,825
Lhotse	Nepal	8426	27,644
Dhaulgiri	Nepal	8172	28,810
Manaslu	Nepal	8165	26,788
Annapurna 1	Nepal	8078	26,504
Gasherbrum (Hidden peak)	Pakistan	8068	26,470
Gosainthan	Tibet Himalayas	8014	26,292

THE FORMATION OF THE HIMALAYAS

Most people do not tend to travel about wondering how hills, mountains or valleys came to be there in the first place. The Himalayas, though, are so high and so significant, that they seem inevitably to beg the question: why are they there? To get the answer, we have to go back a long way.

If you look at a relief map of the area of India and the Himalayas—or better still a satellite photograph—it is obvious that the Himalayas stretch across the top of the Indian 'triangle' where it joins the main Asian landmass. The surface of the Earth is moving around in 'plates', which, over millions of years, can move considerable distances. It is believed that 'India', as a separate island, once lay well south of the equator and gradually moved northwards on its

3. The highest Himalayan peaks, such as the Annapurna group, are well above the permanent snow-line.

plate until, eventually, it collided with the Asian continental mass. The Indian plate began to slide under the Asian plate, but the continuing north-wards and upwards movement, not surprisingly, produced a buckling of the Asian landmass, resulting in the Himalayas and various other mountains and high plateaux. Most non-volcanic mountains were formed in this way, including the Alps, the Rockies and the Atlas mountains, though there are not always two landmasses involved, for a moving plate can lie under the sea.

In fact, the plates are still moving together, and the Himalayas are still rising, though not as fast as they once did. Although the upheavals began about 60 million years ago, some of the most rapid periods of uplifting were relatively recent (geologically speaking)—just a few million years ago. It is believed that the Himalayas rose by about 3000 m (10,000 ft) in a period of a little over a million years, ending about half a million years ago—one of the most dramatic geological events in history. Although they seem so vast to us, and it might seem incredible that they could form in this way, you have to realize that, in proportion to the size of the Earth and these moving continents, they are quite small. Proportionally, they are no more than the tiny wrinkles on the skin of an orange!

As they uplifted, they eroded, and this is why they are so jaggedly beautiful today. It is typical of more recent mountains that they are generally more jagged and sharply-etched, in contrast to the rounded profiles of ancient mountains. One strange product of the rapid uplift and subsequent erosion is the way in which the rivers behave: you would expect the highest mountain range in the world to be a major watershed, with

rivers flowing away on either side of it. But, because the Asian landmass already had an established river system when the continents collided, these rivers continued to flow southwards. As the landmass rose, it was soft enough for the rivers to erode it and keep pace with it, cutting huge gorges as they did so. The Brahmaputra, however, failed to cut its way through, and was forced to make a vast journey to the east around the Himalayas, eventually cutting its way through in north-east Assam, after beginning its journey just west of Nepal!

Consequently, the Himalyas are characterized by deep, steep gorges, where rivers rising on the Tibetan plateau cut their way through them onto the Indian plains. The deepest valley in the world, by some way, lies between the peaks of

4. The complex masses of terraces that cover many Himalayan hillsides are a response to the absence of any land that is not too steep to cultivate without terracing.

Dhaulgiri (8172 m; 28,810 ft) and the Annapurnas (also rising to over 8000 m; 26,250 ft), where the Kali Gandaki cuts through the range on its way from Mustang to the sea. At its lowest point, between the two peaks, the villages on the valley floor are well below 1000 m (3300 ft), so the scale of the valley is immense. Similarly, the Arun gorge, east of Everest, is about 5500 m (18,000 ft) deep, and the headwaters of the Arun are barely a few miles from the course of the Brahmaputra, making 'capture' of the much larger river by the more erosive Arun a likely eventuality.

The rocks of the Himalayas support the theories of their origin. Not surprisingly, they are immensely varied with many metamorphosed rocks as a result of the huge pressures applied during their uplifting. But there are also many limestones, some bearing marine fossils that could only have been formed under the sea, yet which now lie at all elevations virtually to the

5. The massive bulk of Dhaulgiri, towering over the Kali Gandaki—the deepest valley in the world.

highest peaks. It is by no means uncommon to find fossils at 5000 m (16,400 ft) or higher or to be offered them for sale as collected at this height.

PHYSICAL FEATURES

In most respects, the Himalayas are like any other high mountain range, except that they are much higher. In the eastern section, also, they are surprisingly narrow, which inevitably means that they fall very steeply to the south. Glaciers are present in the Himalayas, but generally they are only short in extent because the slopes fall so steeply and the climate lower down is so warm. In the east there are few glaciers of any length, though many, like the Khumbu glacier below Mt Everest, are very impressive by virtue of their bulk. In the west, longer glaciers are more numerous because the mountain range is broader, and the valleys fall less steeply to the warmth of the plains. The Karakoram is especially noted for its glaciers, including the Baltoro glacier, the Hispar glacier, and the Siachen glacier, the longest of them all, which extends about 72 km (45 miles). All of them, however long, have the effect of gouging out the peaks from which they arise, clawing back into the mountains to produce characteristic cirque formations and ultimately shaping peaks where several glaciers work back towards each other.

Boundaries and passes

Generally speaking, the boundary between China, which lies along the whole of the northern slopes of the Himalayas, and the countries along the southern slopes runs along the ridge of highest peaks, as you might expect. Here and there, though, for political or physical reasons, the southern countries encompass little sections of Tibetan plateauland, and these are some of the most fascinating areas that can be visited. Bhutan has a tiny area, Nepal has areas like Mustang and Dolpo, whilst further west, Ladakh is an obvious trans-Himalayan region, though here the chain structure of the range breaks up more, and it is less straightforward to say which is south of the range and which is north.

Despite the general height of the Himalayas, there are numerous passes over them, and a few of them are not particularly high. The great majority are closed to all but the hardiest travellers for part of the winter; and traditionally they have all, of course, been foot passes only, unlike the easy motor-roads that we associate with the word 'pass' in the Alps or Pyrenees. Nevertheless, roads are beginning to appear, and there is an easy pass through the Himalayas along the Sun Kosi, where the 'Chinese road' links Kathmandu with Lhasa. There are also a few much more difficult jeep roads that cross the range, such as the road from Srinagar to Leh, which traverses a pass of 4094 m (16,380 ft) at its highest point.

Himalayan climates

The Himalayas are dominated by a monsoon climate which affects most of the areas that anyone is likely to visit. In fact, it is really only the southern slopes of the range that are directly affected by the summer monsoon, but this comprises all of the main tourist areas, so it is particularly significant, and it dominates the way of life—and the tourist seasons—of the people of these southern slopes.

A monsoon is not like a hurricane or a typhoon, but more like a rain-dominated season. To help understand its importance and significance, it may be helpful to explain briefly why the monsoon happens at all. In fact, the more that is discovered about the process, the more complex it appears to be; but it is relatively easy to distil the essence.

In summer, the great land mass of Asia warms up more quickly than the seas to the south of it. Warm air over the land therefore rises and brings in moisture-laden air from the Indian Ocean, via the Bay of Bengal to the east, or the Arabian Sea to the west. As this air reaches the land it is forced to rise and precipitates its load of moisture as rain. It then continues to rise and is replaced by more air from over the sea.

Gradually, as this cycle continues, the moist air moves further and further inland, eventually reaching the Himalayas (in the case of the Bay of Bengal arm of the monsoon), where it can no longer proceed northwards and is pushed westwards, along the range. This process continues, with moisture-laden winds moving in from the Bay of Bengal, so long as the land remains warmer than the sea. Eventually, as autumn comes, the land mass ceases to be warmer, and the process ceases.

6. Bridges such as this one, built only slightly above winter water levels, are expected to wash away every monsoon, as river levels rise dramatically.

In practice, the monsoon arrives in June or July and ends in about September, though it varies from year to year, and of course it arrives later in the northern and western parts of its area, furthest from the sea. When it does come, it does not produce continuous rain, and there can be long periods without much rain. Like any other rain-bearing wind, its effects are considerably modified by topography. Most rain is deposited on the first significant hills near the sea, and less is deposited further from the sea, or in rain-shadow areas north-west of higher hills. In the Himalayas, there is a general reduction in the rainfall from the monsoon as you go west along the chain, but locally there may be considerable variations. For example, the slopes of the Annapurna massif tend to get more monsoon rainfall than many areas, because the foothills to the south of them are relatively low—so the clouds keep their rain until they hit the Himalayas proper. In other areas high flanking foothills give more protection.

In the extreme west, the effects of the monsoon are barely felt at all. In Srinagar, for example, the monsoon is characterized merely by a rather humid period; the average rainfall in July and August there is only about 120 mm (5 in), compared to 360 mm (14 in) in Delhi, or over 2000 mm (79 in) in Darjeeling, much further east. In the Afghan Hindu Kush, the effects of the monsoon are insignificant, and summer rainfall there is very low.

As you might expect, the Himalayas form a massive and almost totally effective rain-barrier, so that anything to the north of the main range lies in a total rain-shadow with respect to the monsoon. Any trans-Himalayan areas have a quite different climate to the southern slopes, which is primarily a semi-desert climate. They are arid areas, characterized by warm, dry summers, and exceptionally cold, dry winters, with any precipitation then falling as snow. The average rainfall in Leh, for example, is only 6–7 mm per month, with barely more in summer than in winter. Winter temperatures in Leh are very low, with an average minimum of less than $-10°C$ for three months of the year. Consequently their vegetation is quite different, with no developed forest; and the way of life of the people, who are few in number, is quite different too.

The climate, of course, also varies with altitude. Although there are theoretical equations for calculating just how much the temperature drops for every 100 m (328 ft) you go up, in practice much of this is irrelevant. It undoubtedly gets colder as you go up, but in sunny weather you can walk around with shorts and a shirt at very considerable altitudes, as long as you are prepared for the dramatic drop in temperature when the sun goes down, or, to a lesser extent, if you get a cloudy day. This means that you can almost select the temperature of your choice in the Himalayas; and of course the hill stations, developed by the British, were simply a recourse to the cooler fresher air of the hills after the heat of the plains. There are also changes in precipitation with altitude, though since most visitors avoid the rainy season this has little effect on them. The middle altitudes of the mountains receive most rain, and above about 3000–3500 (10,000–11,500 ft), the rainfall declines again as the clouds have shed their loads on the lower slopes.

7. *The highly dramatic, heavily glaciated peak of Macchapucchare ('Fish-tail') is one of the most impressive features of the central Himalayas.*

CHAPTER THREE

The History of the Himalayas

The Himalayas are not a clearly-defined cultural unit in which one can trace definite historical strands leading in a distinct direction. In fact, they could hardly be further from this simplified ideal. The mountainous nature that unifies them into a major geographical feature has also influenced and complicated their history; they act as a major social barrier, a collection of hundreds of isolated valleys, a corridor, a refuge, and, latterly, as an area of tourism and recreation. Also, despite their relative narrowness, they are an immensely long mountain chain, and clearly the mountains of far western Pakistan or Afghanistan have been subject to quite different influences from those of Sikkim or Bhutan. Thus, the historical story is a bitty, fragmented one, with no clear way of telling it and few clear reference points.

The Himalayas as a social barrier

The Himalayas are the highest mountains on Earth, stretching in a huge chain across the whole of the north of the Indian sub-continent. Few easy passes cross them, and ways around them are inevitably long. They form an almost total barrier between two worlds, with the barren, dry, high-altitude Tibetan and Mongolian world to the north, and the low-lying, tropical, fertile, monsoonal Hindu world to the south. The two worlds are so totally different, that it is almost impossible to imagine them meeting. How different it would be if the Himalayas were not there!

Throughout history, 'India' has suffered from endless waves of invading and migrating people, but almost all have come in from the north-west, through the narrow corridor of the Khyber Pass, or from further to the south, rather than over the Himalayas. Minor invasions and movements have taken place through the passes, but the pattern of major movements of people has been totally influenced by the height, and great difficulty, of the Himalayas.

PREHISTORIC TIMES

It is hardly surprising that records of prehistory in the Himalayas are relatively few; or, at least, relatively few have been found and assessed. It is not an easy area in which to carry out fieldwork, and structures from ancient civilizations may have been lost more than is usual because of the regularity of earthquakes in the Himalayas.

The Indus valley is well-known in that it supported an early example of a highly-developed culture, which flourished from around 2500 BC for about a thousand years. The remains of two key cities have been excavated at Mohenjodaro and at Harappa, though no doubt other cities existed. Elsewhere, there is ample evidence of prehistoric cultures throughout the Himalayas, though they were much less well-organized and left fewer remains to be studied. The early widespread people of India, which included those of the Indus Valley, are known as the Dravidian people, but there is also an earlier

strata of aboriginal people who were gradually pushed towards the mountains by later invaders, remaining only as scattered isolated, primitive tribes.

From about 1500 BC, Aryan people began to invade India from the north-west. They originated from the Russian area, and are assumed to have been much more aggressive than the settled, peaceable Dravidians, since the culture of the Indus Valley civilizations disappeared very quickly at the time of the Aryan influxes, though information on what exactly happened is extremely limited. The following period is known as the Vedic period, from the main source of written information on the period, the Vedas. The Aryans, although their power eventually waned, have had a dominant influence on Indian life, and the combination of their beliefs with the pre-existing civilizations led to the development

8. Peaks around Mt Everest—it is hardly surprising that the Himalayas have acted as a major cultural and physical barrier throughout history.

of Hinduism. By about the seventh century BC, the culture could no longer be said to be Aryan, as their power had waned, and they had become absorbed into the existing people, as so many conquerors are.

From about the sixth century BC, Buddhism began to spread. Much of northern India was fragmented into kingdoms, though in the mountains the organization remained more tribal, with kingless assemblies leading loose groups of people. The Licchavis and Sakyas, amongst others, were of this type.

In the sixth century BC, much of the land now known as Pakistan became part of the Persian

empire of Cyrus the Great, later followed by Alexander the Great of Macedonia. Alexander extended his huge empire as far as the north-west of the Indian subcontinent, reaching India in 326 BC, but only remaining for a brief time. His last general left in 317 BC, leaving few traces of the Greek invasion, though trade with Europe was increased, and perhaps a few white-skinned genes were added to the Indian mixture.

The higher hills escaped much of this constant traffic of invaders, whose sights were usually set on the fertile lowlands. There seems to have been a continuing stream of largely uncharted migration into the hills by people seeking to escape the depredations of invaders, and many hill peoples arose from such times of activity.

An important name in the prehistory of the area is that of King, later Emperor, Asoka. He was one of the kings of the Mauryan dynasty, who ruled a large part of northern India. He was a tolerant and thoughtful king, who, during his reign between 269 and 232 BC, greatly extended the influence of Buddhism into the mountains. He had a habit of erecting rock pillars with inscriptions at the furthest places to which his influence extended, so we know that he covered a large area of the Himalayas, from 'Pakistan' to 'Nepal'. Unusually, for that time, he did not force a particular religion on his subjects, and was tolerant of all religions, but spread the word of Buddhism by example.

THE INDIAN STRAND

The history of the southern side of the Himalayas has been largely dominated by the history of India as a whole, though there have been many small-scale influences from the north, and it is clear that the influence of Tibet and

9. Buddhist stupas throughout the Himalayas indicate the strong Buddhist presence, and a long history of Buddhism in the area.

Buddhism increases the higher into the Himalayas you go. So, to try to clarify some of the historical pattern, the history of India—in the wider sense, including present day Pakistan and Bangladesh—has been separated out as it relates to the Himalayas. The histories of Nepal (which was never part of the British Empire), Bhutan and Tibet have remained largely separate from each other, and we shall look at each in turn.

From about AD 320 northern India was ruled by the Gupta dynasty. This was clearly a relatively settled time, and the arts and study of language flourished in peace and prosperity. From about AD 500 onwards, however, the Guptas underwent a decline, and northern India entered a very unstable period, with constant waves of invaders, and constant internal battles. The Huns invaded from central Asia in the fifth and sixth centuries; Kashmir tried to expand into the plains in the eighth century—unsuccessfully; the Gujaras came to dominate the area by the ninth century; while from the tenth century onwards came the first of many Muslim invasions that were to dominate the next six centuries or so. Mahmud of Ghazni began to invade north-west India from Afghanistan, beginning with raids at the end of the tenth century, but expanding into more serious incursions later. The Muslims differed from previous invaders in that they were crusaders, with the intention of killing or converting, and were therefore much less likely to assimilate to the existing culture and society.

For a while, the warrior princes known as the Rajputs were dominant in northern India, in the eleventh and twelfth centuries, but Muslim invasions continued, culminating in the Mogul (or Mughul) invasions under Babur.

THE MOGUL EMPIRE

By the time of Babur's death in 1530 the Mogul empire extended over a vast section of India from its base in Kabul. Apart from a brief period

when Sher Khan ruled northern India (1540–1545), the Moguls were in charge, re-invading and building on Sher Khan's efficient administration and infrastructure. The Mogul king, Akbar (1556–1605), was a tolerant and intelligent leader and conqueror, and his huge empire included Kashmir and much of the southern fringe of the Himalayas. The peak of the Mogul empire was a time of artistic and architectural expansion, with many great buildings (including the Taj Mahal) and gardens (including the famous Srinagar Mogul gardens) created at this time.

In 1498, there was a quietly significant event, when the first Europeans, Portuguese, landed in India. Although this seemed unimportant at the time, the subsequent competition for trade between European nations, and the ultimate dominance of the British, was to have a major effect on the subcontinent. The Mogul empire continued to be strong through the seventeenth century, but after the death of another remark-

10. Donkey and mule trains still transport goods between Tibet and the south side of the Himalayas, though trade patterns have changed since the Chinese took over Tibet.

able king, Aurangzeb, it began to break up during the eighteenth century.

THE BRITISH EMPIRE

The major power that succeeded the Moguls was Britain, though it was not a straightforward nor immediate transition. Initially, they operated as a trading power, and their influence was through the East India Company, though this influence steadily grew. After the Indian Mutiny of 1857–8, direct imperial government began, and the effect on the subcontinent became greater.

The legacies of the British period are many and varied, though the impact on the Himalayas was relatively slight. In many parts of the Himalayas, the British were either excluded or simply chose not to get involved, where their interests were not threatened. Some of the more tangible legacies include roads and communications, the civil service, many Himalayan 'hill stations', and the houseboats on Srinagar's lakes, which the British initiated because they were prevented from owning land locally.

The British period also, of course, led up to independence and partition in 1947, when India assumed self-government, and East and West Pakistan came into being. At the time, this led briefly to massive civil war and bloodshed, especially in the Punjab, as hatred between Muslims and Hindus came into the open, but a more long-lived legacy of this period is the Kashmir problem.

THE KASHMIR STORY

The history of Kashmir has tended to remain separate from that of India throughout much of historical time. After the Moguls declined in power, it became virtually independent for a while before falling to the Afghans in 1756, then to the Sikhs in 1819. In 1846, the British separated Kashmir from Punjab after their war with the Sikhs, and gave Kashmir to General Gulab Singh as a reward for his neutrality during the war.

When the time for partition came, Kashmir could not be simply assigned to one country or another, in view of its particular independent status as a princely state. Thus, it was left to the ruler to decide whether he wished to join Pakistan or India. The Maharajah, Hari Singh, was Hindu, though the greater part of his people were Muslims, which led to an obvious dichotomy. His delay in deciding, probably in the hope of becoming a neutral buffer state, led to an attempted invasion by tribesmen, organized unofficially by Pakistan. However, the tribesmen travelled neither stealthily nor quickly, and Indian troops flew in to aid Hari Singh in resisting both them and the internal revolts. Naturally enough, this meant that Hari Singh

had to opt for joining India, which he did. Thus a state with a large Muslim majority sits uncomfortably in the Indian union, despite its stronger cultural links with Pakistan, and even its geographical links, since roads and rivers run mainly into Pakistan. On several occasions, India has agreed to a referendum, but in each case it has failed to materialize.

The 'Kashmir problem' has continued to be a major bone of contention and hatred between the two countries, and several wars or clashes have resulted in slight movements of the boundary, and the establishment of a 25 km ($15\frac{1}{2}$ mile) wide ceasefire zone, with UN help.

In fact, India's deep involvement with the Kashmir problem probably caused them to fail to notice that the Chinese were building a road across Indian territory into Ladakh. Despite the following conflict, the Chinese retained this area of land behind another ceasefire line, drawn to give a semblance of stability.

MEANWHILE, IN NEPAL . . .

Nepal generally escaped the waves of invaders that were passing through northern India from prehistoric to medieval times, though it was often indirectly affected by refugees, or secondary invaders forced from their homes. At that time, of course, there was no Nepal as such, nor an India, and such boundaries as existed were very different. Most historical records that refer to Nepal refer primarily to the Kathmandu valley, which has always been the nerve centre of the area.

In the fourth century AD, the Kirantis, who ruled the Kathmandu valley, were replaced by the Lichavis, who dominated a peaceful period until the seventh century when arts and crafts flourished. At the time of Amashuvarman, in the seventh century, the king of Tibet was Srong-Tsan-Gampo, who ruled over a huge area, and decided to extend his influence further by marrying princesses from Nepal and China. Amashuvarman acceded to the request and sent his daughter Bhrikuti to Lhasa. She, together with two Chinese princesses who arrived shortly afterwards, apparently succeeded in converting the Tibetan king to Buddhism, and close relations developed between Nepal and Tibet.

A good deal of trade and artistic interchange took place at this time, and Tibet seems to have exercised some form of loose control over Nepal. Strangely enough, Buddhism flourished and became dominant in Tibet, while it waned in Nepal and was later reintroduced from Tibet.

For a while after this the Guptas from northern India extended their power into the Kathmandu valley, though gradually the Mallas (who came originally from the landed gentry of northern India) became dominant, and the Malla dynasty ruled the valley from the late twelfth century onwards, off and on, until the coming of the Gurkhas. This was largely a settled time, with an upsurge in the arts and construction of religious buildings, and it saw a great shift towards Hinduism and the caste system. Gradually, however, the Malla dominance broke down and the valley disintegrated into a number of smaller city-states, each jostling for power at the expense of the others, and it was this disunity and chaos that probably encouraged the Gurkhas to attack the valley.

THE RISE OF THE GURKHAS AND THE SHAH KINGS

The Gurkhas came from the town of Gurkha, in the mountains west of Kathmandu, though they originated in northern India. They had been gradually extending their influence in the hills, until the ninth king, Marbhupal Shah, began to cast envious looks at the green and fertile Kathmandu valley. In 1736, he attacked, but was totally routed by the King of Kathmandu and his highly-trained Newar troops. Marbhupal returned to Gurkha in disarray, and died soon after, but his son, who took over the kingship at the age of twelve, inherited his father's expansionist aims.

Prithwi Narayan Shah—a famous name in Nepalese history—continued to attack the Kathmandu valley, and, though he was unsuccessful at first, his determination and skill, together with the unrest within the valley paid off in the end. His strategy was a gradual affair, picking off the city-states individually, though the critical moment came in 1768 when he took Kathmandu on the day of the Indra Jatra festival, when most of the population was drunk. By the time of Prithwi's death, in 1775, the Gurkhas ruled over much of the area of present-day Nepal, and laid the foundations for its development as a country with their capital in Kathmandu.

The Gurkha kingdom continued to expand after Prithwi's death from its base in Kathmandu, and their armies went as far west as Kashmir, as far east as Sikkim, and into Tibet as far as Shigatse. This led them to contemplate expanding southwards onto the plains, into the area held by the East India Company. This naturally brought them into direct conflict with the British, and finally a full-scale territorial war broke out in 1814. Although an armistice was declared, fighting broke out again, and peace was not finally declared until 1816 when General Ochterlony's troop threatened the Kathmandu valley itself. Bhim Sen (the current ruler) reluctantly gave up ideas of further expansion, and signed the Treaty of Segauli. This was highly significant in that it fixed the boundaries of present-day Nepal, and provided for the recruitment of Nepalese soldiers into the British Army. From then on, close ties developed between Britain and Nepal.

Within Nepal, things began to deteriorate rapidly, and murder and intrigue became commonplace in the seat of power. A period of considerable unrest and unpleasantness culminated, in 1846, with the famous Massacre of the Kot, when Jang Bahadur Rana and his troops massacred many of Nepal's noblemen at the request of the Queen. Shortly afterwards she tried to have Jang killed, and he subsequently

deposed her and installed himself as leader, with the young king Surendra as a figurehead. This marked the start of the Rana regime, which lasted until the return of the Shah kings in 1951. It was an oppressive and closed period, when links with the outside world were cut and the privileged few flourished at the expense of the masses. There were enlightened Rana rulers, and some changes went on during this period, but few Nepalese would have been unhappy with the end of the Rana regime.

In 1951, the Shah kings returned to full power in Nepal. This was, without doubt, a popular change, though it took some years before the relationship between the monarchy and the government settled down. From 1963 onwards, Nepal's internal politics have been stable, as the world's only constitutional Hindu Monarchy, and there was little sign of any change until

11. Ghandrung village lies in the heart of 'Gurkha' country.

recently. In 1990, however, unrest forced the first changes towards democracy.

SIKKIM

Sikkim forms only a tiny part of the Himalayas (7300 sq km; 2819 sq miles) and is, in any case, now part of India. However, it merits more than a passing mention because of its long history as an independent state, and because of its more direct links with Tibet, Bhutan and Buddhism than the areas further west along the chain.

The indigenous people of Sikkim are known as the Lepchas (see p 48), who, together with the long-established Magars and Tsongs, made up the bulk of Sikkim's population at the time of the takeover by India. From about the thirteenth century onwards, there was a considerable and generally peaceful immigration of Bhotia (or Bhutia) people from the Kham area of Tibet, who mainly settled in the midland valleys to become farmers. In the latter half of the nineteenth century, there was a major influx of people from Nepal, including people from the Newar, Gurung, Tamang and Sherpa races, who settled at various altitudes in Sikkim, according to what they were used to. The hill people, especially the Tamangs (see p 43), brought with them the techniques of terracing, so familiar in Nepal, and later arrivals from the Nepalese lowlands brought the Hindu religion.

In the mid-eighteenth century, Sikkim fought a series of wars with Bhutan, followed by a series of struggles with Nepal under the Gurkha kings, who were trying to expand westwards. Nepal came to occupy part of Sikkim, but they relinquished some of the territory in 1793 and the remainder in 1816 as a result of the Treaty of Segauli. In 1839, the British East India Company obtained Darjeeling from Sikkim for use as a health resort and hill station (still clearly visible in its architecture and colonial atmosphere). As the British became established, they sought to annexe various parts of Sikkim, which led ultimately to several struggles, culminating in the defeat of the Sikkimese and the signing of an Anglo-Sikkimese treaty in 1861. This recognized Sikkim's sovereignty and position here as a buffer state, but granted various concessions to the British.

12. The chain of massive dzongs *in Bhutan, such as this one at Punakha, are a visible reminder of the unifying influence of Ngawang Namgyal.*

In 1890, the Tibetans began to invade Sikkim from the north, but ceased after prolonged discussions with Britain. After Indian independence in 1947, Sikkim signed a treaty with the new government, making Sikkim an Indian protectorate. This marked a period of considerable internal disunion, as infant political groupings argued about their attitude towards India. Finally, after a long period of unrest, India annexed Sikkim in 1975, and brought her into the Indian Union as the 22nd state, with the deposition of the ruling Chogyal and the commencement of direct rule by India.

BHUTAN

In Bhutan, as in much of the rest of the eastern Himalayas, history and religion are closely intertwined, with Buddhism as the pre-eminent religion. Sadly, the history of Bhutan is not as well documented as it once was, for most of the irreplaceable Namthar (ancient printing blocks) of the national archive were destroyed in fires in 1828 and 1832, followed by the loss of many more in an earthquake in 1896, followed by another fire. Almost the whole of the historical record of Bhutan under Buddhism had been destroyed.

In the seventh century AD, Bhutan was an area in which the animist/mystical religion of Bonism was practised. In 747, or thereabouts, the revered religious leader Guru Padma Sambhava came from Tibet and introduced Buddhism to Bhutan. (It is interesting that Buddhism reached Bhutan, and Sikkim, by a circuitous route from Nepal to Tibet, then back across the Himalayas, rather than directly from India, indicating the direction in which the connections of these eastern countries lay.) Sambhava is also known to the Bhutanese as Guru Rimpoche, and he is still highly revered there. His teachings were so precious that they were known as *Termas* or treasures, to be safeguarded and hidden in difficult times. He is also credited with many miracles and extraordinary events. Bhutan has

remained Buddhist ever since, although the type of Buddhism has changed under the influence of emissaries of different sects in Tibet. For much of its medieval period, Bhutan seems to have been distinguishable as a vague entity, within similar boundaries to the present ones, but with no clear leading force, and numerous separate languages and subdivisions of Buddhism. In the seventeenth century, however, a lama called Ngawang Namgyal appeared on the scene and changed the course of Bhutanese history.

In Tibet, the Gelugpa sect of Buddhism was becoming aggressively dominant, and many lamas of the Drukpa sect were forced to flee or submit. Many found their way to Bhutan. One such lama was Namgyal. He arrived in Bhutan in 1616, at a time when there were no laws, no single dominant religion, and no central authority, yet by the time of his death in 1651, the whole of western Bhutan was under one government, and five years later the whole country had one government and one religion—Drukpa Buddhism.

Namgyal achieved this by a mixture of foresight, energy, politics and religion. One of his great unifying achievements, and one which is still a great feature of Bhutan today, was the construction of a series of massive *dzongs* (fortress monasteries) in all the valleys of western Bhutan, which rapidly became focal points for the civil and religious life of each region. When Tibet invaded Bhutan from the north in 1639, it was Namgyal who succeeded in uniting the disparate Bhutanese and routing the Tibetans, and this success led him to adopt the title of Shabdung, the First. He thus effectively became the temporal and spiritual ruler of all Bhutan.

His influence did not last long after his death, in some senses, since no suitable successor was found, and the country gradually deteriorated into disunity, though retaining its boundaries and identity. By the eighteenth and early nineteenth centuries, the Bhutanese as a whole were well-enough organized to begin thinking about

*13. Tibetan faces are a common sight now on the
southern slopes of the Himalayas—the result of
much cross-migration in the last 30 years.*

expansion, and as their efforts turned south-wards, so they came into contact with the British. In 1773, one clash, which the Bhutanese lost, led to the signing of a peace treaty and a period of increased contact between the two countries. In the early decades of the nineteenth century, though, Bhutan began to expand into a disorganized Assam, gradually gaining control of many strategic areas. When the British came to occupy Assam, another series of Anglo-Bhutanese clashes resulted, culminating in the Treaty of Sinchaula, which marked an end to hostilities and the start of a new relationship.

Internally, Bhutan's lack of a single strong leader continued until 1903, when one of the dominant state governors, Ugyen Wangchuck, decided to assist the British on a mission to Tibet, where he helped to negotiate an agreement in Lhasa. On his return in 1907, Wangchuck was appointed hereditary ruler of Bhutan, with the title of Druk Gyalpo—Precious Ruler of the Dragon people. Ugyen was a strong and capable leader, who was succeeded by his son Jigme Wangchuck, and the family have remained as Bhutan's ruling royal family ever since.

THE TIBETAN SIDE

Tibet has been mentioned at times as a dominating force on all the countries mentioned, and it is clear that there has been a strong religious and military presence in Tibet for a very long time. An early Tibetan king, Srong-Tsan-Gampo, who ruled in the seventh century AD, has already been mentioned for his marriage to a Nepalese princess. He ruled over a huge area, but his descendants continued to expand the Tibetan empire at an extraordinary rate, such that at one time it extended into Kashmir, Sikkim, Bhutan, Nepal, Burma and China proper, as well as far to the north. There seemed to be a constant stream of border skirmishes, and it is by no means clear

where the wealth to fuel this expansion came from.

Since that time Tibet's fortunes have waxed and waned, with much of the pattern irrelevant to the Himalayan area. At some time or other, large areas of the northern Himalayas, and especially trans-Himalayan areas like Ladakh and Dolpo, have come under Tibetan religious and political influence, and most such areas have retained their Buddhist beliefs.

In 1950, soon after any threat of British involvement had been removed by Indian independence, China began the process of 'liberating' Tibet. Although it may be generally accepted that the pre-existing Tibet was far from being a perfect society, most people believe that the Chinese invasion of Tibet was unwarranted and highly damaging to a unique and historic culture and people. The struggle against occupation has continued ever since, resulting eventually in an easing of the hard-line policy from around 1979 onwards, though more recent events in China, in 1989, may provoke a harder line again.

The effects of Chinese occupation on the Himalayas has been definite, and generally detrimental. Patterns of trade for countries like Nepal and Bhutan have changed considerably; road building for purely military purposes has destroyed the isolation of many areas, and many of the larger species of wildlife have been wantonly shot for food or sport by Chinese soldiers. Greatly intensified sheep-farming, organized by the Chinese, has reduced the grazing and caused further dwindling of many rare grazing species such as blue sheep and Tibetan gazelle, and the animals that prey upon them, like the snow leopard. There can be few good features of the grey and cruel Chinese communist culture in Tibet to set against the colourful, historic and unique nature of the country that preceded it.

CHAPTER FOUR

The People of the Himalayas and their Festivals

The resident peoples of the Himalayas are an incredible mixture of races, with a wide range of origins, complicated by centuries or millennia of separate development in isolated valleys. Aboriginal people have retreated upwards and away from centres of population, invaders have come and gone, refugees have fled into the area and settled, while other groups have moved quite short distances from their homelands to find somewhere more prosperous. The result is not something that can be encapsulated in a brief chapter in a book. Even the broad definitions of people, such as Indo-Aryan and Tibeto-Burman, become difficult to apply universally because of the complexity of the area.

However, some general patterns can be distinguished, for what they are worth. In religious terms—which have some relation with racial origins, but not a complete one—the western Himalayas from Afghanistan to Kashmir are primarily Muslim, with an admixture of other religions to the east, and with pockets of other types, such as the Kalash people of West Pakistan; from Himachal Pradesh eastwards, there is a general pattern to the effect that Hindus live at the lower and middle levels of the mountains, whilst Buddhist people live at the highest levels, and there are often mixed Buddhist-Hindu groups (i.e. believing something of both religions) somewhere in between. The further east you go in the Himalayas, the more prevalent Buddhism becomes. These patterns relate primarily to the early Muslim invasions from the west, a constant flow of religious ideas and occasional military campaigns from Buddhist Tibet in the north, and the strong Hindu pressure from India in the south, declining eastwards. The Buddhist-Hindu division relates roughly to an ethnic and linguistic division, though not wholly, as many conversions to one or other religion have occurred through the centuries.

Religion is not simply important in the lives of virtually all Himalayan peoples—it pervades everything about their lives, and it is impossible to separate the ordinary things of daily life from religion. Festivals provide one particularly visible aspect of religion, since virtually all are of religious significance, but it does not give a full impression of how religion affects the daily lives of the people. Most Himalayan residents live, or have lived, so close to the elements, with constant difficulties posed by floods, earthquakes, landslides, drought, famine, wild animals or whatever, that they have inevitably developed a close respect for the natural world. Their religions are often a focus for this respect, especially in the more primitive people still practising ancient spirit worship.

It is not easy for the average traveller to become more than superficially aware of the different races present in the Himalayas. On a typical trek from Lamosangu to Everest, for

14. The 'chariot' of Red Machendranath—part of a major Newar festival held in Kathmandu.

example, one passes through the territory of a number of different peoples, but most trekkers are unaware of it, except when they enter upper Sherpa-land (Khumbu). The vast amount of new information that comes at the first-time visitor, the confusion caused by people who are just passing through (including your own Sherpas and porters if you have them), and also the lack of close contact with local people, can easily lead the trekker into failing to see the changes. It is well worth observing the dress of the people, their facial characteristics, their hair, the style of building, and any other features, as well as asking your Sherpas, or anyone who speaks your language, about the country you are passing through. This way, you can soon start to pick up the tell-tale signs of changes in race as you pass through different areas, though the change is by no means always abrupt or clear-cut.

The following section selects a number of better-known, significant, or especially interesting groups and races that occur in the Himalayas. It is not, of course, a comprehensive list, nor are the divisions between people always as clear as this separate treatment implies.

PEOPLE OF THE WESTERN HIMALAYAS

The *Kalash* are a tiny group of people, barely 3000 strong, but of particular interest as a tribe of 'non-believers' surrounded by a sea of Muslims. They live in three valleys on Pakistan's extreme western border, not far from Chitral, and are clearly different physically from those around them in that they are primarily light-skinned, with fairish hair and blue, green or grey eyes. This has led to persistent rumours and suggestions that they descend from Alexander the Great's troops, though anthropologists generally discount this idea. They have no written language, an animistic religion, and a

15. Family members arriving to celebrate a wedding in a high Himalayan village, Langtang.

belief that they emanated from 'Tsiam', though no-one has worked out where this is. They celebrate various festivals, including Chaomos, at the winter solstice, and Phoo at autumn harvest.

The *People of Hunza* became famous a while ago as the residents of a putative Shangri-La, where great longevity was commonplace, due largely to eating apricots. These apricots are now widely exported. Sadly, though there was truth in all aspects of the story, it was not entirely accurate, and subsequently the isolation of this extraordinary area has ended, with the coming of the Karakoram highway. The Hunzas themselves divide roughly into two groups in lower and upper Hunza, with different languages. All are Muslims, of the Ismaili sect, dating from the earliest movements of Muslims into this area, and they had a rich separate cultural tradition, with numerous festivals. More recently, the Karakoram highway has hastened the process of homogenization drastically. The Upper Hunza people have more cultural affinities with Tibet, though the area is a complex melting-pot.

The *Kashmiris* are the people of the area round Srinagar in Kashmir. They are of central Asian origin, and generally different in appearance from Indians of further south, though because Kashmir has been accessible and popular for some while, a good deal of admixture has taken place. They are mainly Muslim, and have a reputation for dishonesty and conniving both amongst Indians and visitors, the subject of many sayings such as: 'The Kashmiris are so fond of the truth that they refuse to part with it'! The reputation is probably not fully justified. They no longer have a strong cultural identity, though there are more isolated tribal groups in the area, speaking different languages and retaining strong cultural traditions.

16. Bands playing at the Red Machendranath festival in Patan in May. The wheels of the 'chariot' bearing the god are on the left. Nepal.

The *Ladakhis* are the inhabitants of Ladakh, the northernmost area of the states of Jammu and Kashmir. Although part of India now, the area is almost totally Tibetan in character and religion. The people themselves are racially very like Tibetans, and the traditional language is a form of Tibetan, though not suprisingly this is changing now, since the Indian languages are of much more use. The area is thickly covered with monasteries, many of them very ancient and beautiful, which are the centres of the Buddhist faith in the area (though there are also many Muslims). Regular festivals take place in these monasteries, especially in winter, and family festivals take place for births and marriages. The Ladakhis are an attractive, friendly, outgoing people, with great dignity and honesty, like most people of Tibetan origin.

PEOPLE OF THE CENTRAL HIMALAYAS

The *Newars* of Nepal are the traditional indigenous people of the Kathmandu valley. They are a large and influential group, numbering nearly half a million, most of whom live around Kathmandu, spreading out into the surrounding area. They are racially mixed, of obscure ancient origins, but culturally very distinct. Strangely, they may be either Buddhist or Hindu, and probably they were once wholly Buddhist, but have been gradually converted to Hinduism, though there is no antagonism between the two

17. Girls from Mustang, in the far north of Nepal, share a joke in Manang village on the upper Kali Gandaki.

groups. In fact, many temples and festivals have elements of each religion. Many of the great ceremonies of the Kathmandu valley are essentially Newar, and they are likely to become familiar to any visitor, especially in spring and autumn. The ceremonies of Indra Jatra, Gai Jatra and Rath Jatra, together with many more general ceremonies such as the Hindu Tihar and Dasain, or Buddha's birthday, are all celebrated in the Kathmandu valley. It makes for added interest to be in Kathmandu during a major festival, which is well worth attending, except for when you are urgently awaiting a trekking permit, since this may then be delayed until 'the day after tomorrow . . .'

The *Tamangs* are primarily Nepalese, extending their home area from central Nepal as far as the hills of West Bengal. They are people of the middle and higher hills, familiar to anyone who goes trekking in Nepal as the backbone of the armies of porters that accompany trek groups and expeditions. There are between half a million and a million, making them one of the largest ethnic groups in Nepal. Their origins lie in Tibet (Tamang means horse trader in Tibetan), but they have clearly been in Nepal a long time. They are primarily farmers, who develop their tremendous load carrying abilities early in life in response to the demands of their environment. The Tamang villages are characteristically neat, with stone-paved roads, stone-built resting-places, often under a pipal tree, and stone-built two-storey houses with wood or slate roofs. They are normally devout Buddhists and prayer flags, prayer walls and shrines are a feature of Tamang areas, though some lower-living people

18. The neat, well-organized village of Lumle, below Annapurna.

may be Hindu; as a group they may celebrate Hindu festivals.

The *Gurungs* are a large and relatively well-known group from the mountains around Annapurna in central Nepal, who have formed one of the main races from which the 'Gurkha' regiments are recruited. (Gurkhas are not a specific race or nation, but a mixture of several hill tribes, including Magars and Gurungs, from central Nepal.) They are farmers, both growing

19. A Gurung girl, near Ghandrung, Nepal.

crops and keeping sheep, and they tend to live at slightly higher altitudes than their near-neighbours, the Magars. Typically, their origins are obscure, though they have definite Mongolian features. It is from the Gurungs that the 'honey-hunters of Nepal' come, recently photographed and described so vividly in articles in the world's press, though it seems that the tradition is about

*20. In hill villages in the Himalayas, all members of
the family carry loads from an early age!*

21. *A Sherpani porter, still elegant after a day's load-carrying at high altitude. These 'Lady Sherpas' frequently carry their children as well as a load, and do their knitting as they walk!*

22. *Wheat-threshing in November, Gurung village.*

to end. The *Magars* are culturally distinct, though similar to the Gurungs in many ways, living slightly further east and at slightly lower altitudes. Their houses are beautiful oval or circular constructions, white-washed or red-washed, except in the east of their range.

Without a doubt, the best-known of all Himalayan people are the *Sherpas*. Until the early 1950s they were unknown outside their own region, but now their name is synonymous with toughness, cheerfulness and strength, and they have had makes of van, rucksacks, trekking companies, and all sorts of things named after them!

They live in a relatively confined area of Nepal south of Mount Everest, known as Solu-Khumbu, though somewhat less distinctive Sherpas live in other areas. It is the high-altitude Sherpas, from Khumbu, who live in villages at around 3–4000 m (10–13,000 ft), who have become famous as mountaineers, guides and companions. Their origins were undoubtedly in Tibet, and they are known to have crossed the high passes into Nepal some 3–400 years ago in several migrations. They are a lively and outgoing people, with immense energy and fitness, liked by everyone who comes into contact with them. Basically, their way of life is agricultural, growing crops and keeping yaks, but they are also traders and, increasingly, the young men act as guides and leaders; many spend up to half the year based in Kathmandu, returning home for the summer agricultural activities with much-needed extra cash.

Sherpa festivals are famous affairs, perhaps partly because they have been more accessible than those of some mountain groups. They are strongly Buddhist, and the festivals are centred around the monasteries, or *gompas*. Festivals include Lhosar, the Tibetan New Year in February, when Sherpas have traditionally come home to work in the fields; Dumdze (or Dumje) in the middle of summer, during the monsoon; and the famous Mani Rimdu festivals, which attract so many visitors. These last festivals take place twice a year, in May at Thame and in November at Tengboche. The Tengboche festival takes place at the height of the autumn trekking season, so that many visitors can attend parts of this spectacular affair, in addition to the hundreds of Sherpas. Tengboche, in the shadow of Everest, and one of the most beautiful places in the world, is the most important monastery in the area because of the presence there of a learned reincarnated Lama as abbot. Sadly, the monastery was recently seriously damaged by fire and money is still being raised for its restoration.

A vague term that is often encountered with reference to people occurring almost anywhere in the Himalayas is the *Bhotias* (or *Bhutias*). This is a general, and not very specific, term for groups of people who have come over from Tibet to settle somewhere on the southern slopes, almost anywhere between Bhutan and Kashmir. Only some such groups tend to be called Bhotias—much older settlers, like the Sherpas, may have their own names, whilst refugees from the Chinese takeover tend to be referred to as Tibetan refugees. The term tends to refer more to people like the villagers of Langtang, in Nepal, who are known to have come over from Tibet (probably the Kyirong area) several generations ago.

PEOPLE OF THE EASTERN HIMALYAS

The *Lepchas* are the long-established people of Sikkim. They have no written or oral tradition of migration, and there are no records of such, so it is probable that they are the aboriginal people of Sikkim. They speak a Tibeto-Burman language, with a more recently-devised script, and their religion is Buddhism, although there are elements of the pre-Buddhist religion—Bonism—

23. Himalayan villages blend organically into their environment.

24. *Autumn harvest time, near Pokhara, Nepal.*

25. *The bridegroom at a 'Bhotia' wedding, Langtang valley.*

in their present-day worship. The population of Sikkim has become diluted by numerous incomers from all directions, and the Lepchas are now a relatively small group.

The *Bhutanese people* are not a single, ethnically distinct, race, though they are far less culturally diverse than the Nepalese. The two oldest-established groups, who now make up about half of the population, are the *Sharchops* and the *Ngalops*. The Sharchops are believed to be the oldest inhabitants of the area; they are of Indo-Mongolian type, though their origins are unclear, with somewhere in Tibet as the most likely source. At present, they live mainly in eastern Bhutan, in the more remote areas. The Ngalops are the descendants of more recent

26. An archery contest outside the dzong. Archery is the national sport of Bhutan, popular everywhere. The participants always wear the national dress, as seen here.

immigrants from Tibet who entered Bhutan at various periods from the ninth century onwards, bringing their customs and religion with them. They now live mainly in the west and centre of the country, which is the centre of Bhutanese government. These two groups are sometimes known collectively as the Bhutias or Bhotes (i.e. of Tibetan origin). The remainder of Bhutan's population is made up largely of Nepalese, living mainly in the south-west of the country.

Wherever you travel in the Himalayas, except in parts of the largest towns, you will find that the people have strong traditions and religious beliefs. As visitors to this unique area, it is up to us to respect these traditions and cultures in every way possible; they are under enough threat

27. *Masked monk dancer at a festival at Wangdiphodrang Dzong, Bhutan.*

from changes going on all around them without any added burden from thoughtless visitors.

CHAPTER FIVE

Visiting the Himalayas

For many people, a visit to the Himalayas is a once-in-a-lifetime dream, to be saved up for and savoured many years in advance. The possibilities for visiting the Himalayas have greatly increased recently, and access has grown easier, such that many more people are now coming to the Himalayas for one reason or another. This chapter is intended as a general guide on when to visit and how to get there. Although obviously it cannot be a comprehensive guide, it should help to avoid some of the pitfalls and mistakes that could occur. Further details of particular facets of the Himalayas, and particular activities, are given in more detail in succeeding chapters.

WHEN TO VISIT

Timing is critical to the success of a visit to the Himalayas. The seasonal changes are very strongly marked, and generally fairly predictable, so with a little advance planning you can select the conditions you require. For most visiting purposes, the Himalayas can be separated into the monsoonal eastern area, with its exceptionally wet summers, and the non-monsoonal western Himalayas (see Chapter 2), and each has different requirements.

The eastern Himalayas (comprising the Indian Himalayas east of Kashmir, together with the whole of Nepal, Sikkim, Bhutan and Assam) are strongly influenced by the monsoon, giving them very wet, humid summers and generally dry winters. However, for visitors, the seasons

are slightly more complicated, and it is worth considering them in more detail.

For the general visitor, the best time of year is almost certainly autumn (i.e. October and November and just into December). This period follows closely after the monsoon, and everywhere looks fresh and green, the air is clear and clean, and the white-capped mountains look to be just a few miles away in the clear air. Four months of heavy rain has a considerable effect on the appearance of the country. At this time of the year it is, in general, neither too hot in the lowlands nor too cold in the mountains, and the sun shines from clear blue skies for most of the time. Probably the most reliable month for weather is November, and I have trekked to Everest, Langtang, Annapurna and many other areas at this time of year, to heights of over 5500 m (18,000 ft), with continuous blue skies, except for a few days of mist close to Everest. There is, perhaps, evidence of a very slight shift towards showery autumns, in keeping with wider changes in weather patterns, and my last autumn visit was marked by heavier rainfall than usual. But none the less it is an incredible time to visit this section of the Himalayas.

Towards the end of November, it begins to get very cold at night in the higher areas—though still usually very pleasant in the day—and December becomes colder still, though generally still clear and sunny. In the lowland or mid-height towns, such as Kathmandu or Darjeeling, December is very pleasant, with cold misty

mornings, but frequent warm sunny days. In the new year, a period of greater snowfall and generally more unsettled weather begins. This is the coldest period, and it is also rather more unsettled, with a greater chance of rain, snow or cloud, though it is still relatively dry compared to the summer. Lower peaks which had turned grey or brown through the summer and autumn turn white again, though snow rarely lies for long below about 2500 m (8200 ft). Trekking in the hills at this time is perfectly possible, though you need to be well-prepared for cold weather, and many passes will become closed by snow to normal travellers.

Spring is another favourable time to visit the eastern Himalayas, from March through to May. The weather is generally good at this period, though it can get uncomfortably warm in the lowlands by May, and the latter part of the period is characterized by periodic showery,

28. Winter makes trekking at high altitude difficult, because passes are blocked, and ordinary trails may be difficult. Early March, at 4550 m (15,000 ft).

thundery weather.

Spring is a good time to be almost anywhere, and the Himalayas are no exception, with crops growing strongly everywhere, many shrubs in flower in the forests, and blue irises and primulas starting to appear in the high pastures. It is *the* time for seeing rhododendrons, and whole hillsides can be ablaze with these shrubs, which you miss entirely if you go in autumn. There are also masses of birds, in their smartest breeding plumage, wherever you go. The disadvantage in going in spring, apart from the slightly more unsettled and thundery weather, is the thin dusty haze that pervades the atmosphere. This spreads up in clouds from the hot, dry, dusty plains of India and gradually obscures the views, so that in

spring you rarely get good views of the mountains from lower down. It is not a thick, choking dust, but more of a dull haze. If you are trekking, you will notice that above about 3000 m (9850 ft), the haze begins to thin out and your views of the mountains become much clearer. At the same time, you can see the band of hazy dust extending away over the lowlands, and you feel glad that you have come up out of it!

By May, the air begins to become dull and heavy in the lowlands and some areas will suffer thunderstorms. At first, they come only in the evenings, but gradually their frequency increases. Some areas suffer much more than others, depending upon the juxtaposition of hot plains and cold mountains; the Pokhara area, for example, which lies just south of the Annapurna massif in Nepal, suffers greatly from early summer thunderstorms; the hot lowlands are particularly close to the mountains here, and there is considerable buildup of turbulence.

Summer is monsoon time, essential for the crops but much less welcome for the visitor. It arrives some time in June, or into July in the western parts of this section, and its coming is eagerly welcomed. This period is not a time when a visit to the Himalayas can be recommended, especially if you only have one opportunity to go, unless you have specific reasons for going then. The rainfall in the monsoon period, from June to September, is very considerable throughout most of this area, and it is particularly heavy in the east. Darjeeling, for example, receives 2500 mm of rainfall (about 100 inches) in the monsoon. However, it does not rain all the time, and many days start clear, briefly, before clouding up. There are periods with no rain at all for several days, or even weeks, but generally speaking the whole period is characterized by humid, rainy weather.

29. Kathmandu is the base for a vast number of treks and excursions in Nepal. Rani Pokhari at dawn.

If you are planning to travel in the hills, the monsoon has other relevant effects, too. Paths become difficult and slippery and a great deal of erosion goes on, with whole paths disappearing down a soggy hillside, barring your route. Some of the bridges are built in the expectation that monsoon floods will wash them away, and many otherwise easy routes are interrupted by a foaming torrent with no bridge. The other big problem in the monsoon season is the leeches; these invertebrates mature in the rainy season in vast numbers, and it is impossible to walk anywhere in the hills without collecting a good few of them on your legs. This alone puts most people off!

However, if you wish to see the high-altitude flowers at their best, see all the bird species breeding, look at the summer crops, or see any of the other things that only go on in summer, then you have little choice but to go in the monsoon.

So in summary, October–November and March–April are the best times to visit most areas of the Himalayas east of Kashmir, with the balance lying in favour of autumn because of the very settled weather, the clear air, the colours of the land, and the succession of festivals going on.

Western Himalayas: For the purpose of this chapter, the western Himalayas include Kashmir and everything to the west of it, such as Chitral, Gilgit and the Hindu Kush. Because this area lies virtually outside the monsoon belt (and is quite unaffected by it in the north and west of the area), the weather pattern, and thus the times for optimum visiting, are quite different.

Easily the most popular season for Kashmir (including Ladakh) and westwards from there, is the summer, i.e. June until September. This is an excellent time to be in the area, with good, warm weather, lots of flowers, easier access, and for

30. Autumn is the time for clear views of the mountains and reliable sunny weather throughout most of the Himalayas.

many, especially residents of India, it is the best time to be away from the heat and rain of lowland monsoon India. Consequently, though it is the best time in most respects, it is also the busiest, and key areas like Srinagar do become very crowded.

Autumn is a good time for visiting this area, and there are many fewer people, though the autumns are colder here than further south and east and access over higher passes becomes difficult by November. For most visitors, October marks the end of the season for visiting the higher parts of the western Himalayas, though winter visits are possible, and they may be exciting in other ways. Kashmir has good autumn colour and plenty of places remain open for visitors, so there is no problem here, though flights become a little unreliable by late November, and snow is likely from then on.

Winter is not considered to be a good time to visit much of the western Himalayan areas (unless specifically for skiing—see Chapter 9), though possibilities do exist if you are persistent and not on a tight schedule. A trip at this time does allow you to see the local people relatively undisturbed by tourists, and more remote areas, such as Leh, are usually completely free from visitors. The northerly and higher areas are extremely cold in winter. The weather may often be sunny and bearable during the day, but night temperatures drop to very low levels. The biggest problem is access, and most road passes are closed during the winter for at least some of the time. It is possible to fly into the higher areas in winter, including Srinagar and even Leh, but you cannot be sure of getting there when you want to, nor—perhaps more importantly— getting out when you want to. I have had to cancel a trip to Kashmir in early December because of heavy snow, and have heard of people getting marooned in Leh for two weeks more than they intended. The flights will be cancelled at very short notice if weather reports are poor, and this is really in everyone's interests.

Spring, which starts a little later here than further south and east, is a good time to visit. From late March or April onwards, depending on elevation and latitude, the snow clears, the fruit trees come into blossom, and the passes begin to open up. You are unlikely to be able to drive to Leh by then, but certainly the lower areas are easily accessible, quite quiet, and very attractive.

By June, you begin to move into the warmer weather, which is starting to become unbearable on the plains, and the peak season starts again.

ACCESS TO THE HIMALAYAN REGION

Access within the Indian sub-continent is mainly by railway, by road (especially by unpowered means), and, for tourists and wealthier residents, by air, with walking as the primary means of travel over shorter distances.

In the Himalayas, though, things are rather different. Railways are virtually irrelevant for getting into the mountains, and the only remotely useful lines are the Indian branch-lines to Siliguri (quite close to Darjeeling), and the lines up into north-west India, to the edge of Kashmir state, though both leave considerable road journeys before you reach real mountain areas, apart from the occasional small-gauge line you can transfer to, such as the one to Simla.

Roads are being steadily built and improved, but you cannot regard them in the same way as those in Europe or North America. Even where they are shown on the map—and there are huge areas that have none—they may often be very slow and hazardous, and in a poor state of repair. Completely new roads may have a reasonable surface (though they rarely stay in this state for long), but they are still extremely slow because they are narrow, incredibly tortuous, and frequently blocked by landslides, snow, water or other hazards. If trying to estimate the length of a journey by vehicle in the Himalayas, you can reckon on at least four times what you might expect, more if travelling by bus,

and distances on maps are gross underestimations because of the huge number of bends to be negotiated.

However, roads can get you to all the relevant major towns of the Himalayas, where you can start a more adventurous journey on foot; and normally you will have to visit a major town before you start, to get permits, etc. There is a remarkable road into Ladakh, reaching the capital town, Leh, from Srinagar in Kashmir, and also the extraordinary Karakoram highway running right from the north of Pakistan to the Chinese border at the Khunjerab pass. Further east, the roads are less adventurous, but Kathmandu, Pokhara and Darjeeling are all readily accessible, and small roads lead a little further into the mountains from Kathmandu, while the Chinese road from Kathmandu to Lhasa is now a convenient take-off point for treks to Everest and parts of east Nepal.

31. Bridges such as this are commonplace throughout the Himalayas. They are perfectly safe during the dry season, but dangerous or non-existent in the monsoon, causing many trails to be impassable.

Luckily, though, the vast majority of the areas in the Himalayas remain roadless, and are accessible only on foot.

In some areas, access is greatly extended by the provision of small airstrips, accessible by small or medium-sized planes. Many places also have rough helicopter landing pads, though the helicopter is too expensive a vehicle to provide a regular means of transport, and it is mainly used for emergencies, wealthy visitors' rapid sight-seeing tours, and for supplies in some remote areas. The airstrips, however, certainly allow access to many more remote areas than the roads do, and of course the journey is much quicker,

though not always more reliable. Nepal probably has the best-developed network of flights,
based on STOL (short take-off and landing)
planes, and these give access to such places as
Lukla and Tengboche, very close to Everest,
Jomsom, and Jumla in western Nepal, which are
all well away from roads.

In India, you can fly to Srinagar in Kashmir,
Leh in high Ladakh, Bagdogra for Darjeeling,
though large areas of the Indian Himalayas are
not served by significant airstrips. In Pakistan,
there are flights to Chitral, Gilgit and Skardu,
which can save considerable time, though these
are all accessible by road. In fact, seats for
visitors are very limited, and flights are very
unpredictable owing to the weather, so you may
find yourself taking longer than the road trip
anyway. In Bhutan, the main airport is at Paro,
taking flights in from India.

*32. The Taschichodzong in Bhutan, one of the
main sights seen by virtually all visitors to the
country.*

Apart from these various routes, the main
means of access for everyone in the Himalayas is
on foot, and there is a vast network of footpaths
of various grades linking all villages and crossing
many high passes. Pack animals, including
donkeys, mules, horses and yaks, are used,
though by no means everywhere, and in many
parts the most important beast of burden is man.
I could recommend that anyone who is modera-
tely fit, or capable of getting fit, tries at least a
brief period of walking in the mountains as the
only real way of getting to see what they are like
and how the people live and work. Chapters 7
and 8, on trekking in the Himalayas, give more
details of how and where you can go.

CHAPTER SIX

The Naturalist in the Himalayas

(For the section on Wildlife Reserves and National Parks see p 128.)

For the naturalist, the Himalayas are one of the most exciting places in the world to visit, while for the less specialized traveller, the wealth of interesting and vivid flowers, birds and other forms of life soon draws them under its spell. Many organized trips to the Himalayas have natural history as their prime interest, reflecting both the wealth of things to be seen, and the degree of interest in natural history.

It is not possible to cover adequately the range of natural life to be found in the Himalayas, since the number of species, and the possibilities for seeing them, are both vast. For example, the total number of species of flowering plants in the Himalayas (excluding all lower plants, such as lichens, mosses and fungi) is estimated to be about 9000, depending upon how widely the definition of the area is drawn. Thus the aim of this chapter is more to explain the background to the natural history, to pick out some highlights, and to draw attention to the places that are of especial interest to the naturalist.

There are now a number of reasonable guide books covering a high proportion of the birds, mammals and flowers that you can expect to see (see Bibliography), and the specialized naturalist is advised to obtain these. Not surprisingly, however, information on the less well-known groups such as insects and other invertebrates, fungi, lichens, reptiles and so on, is much more difficult to obtain. It is well worth visiting any museum, botanical garden or zoo in main Himalayan towns if you are passing through. These are useful before a trip, to give an idea of what may be seen, but they are also useful afterwards to help to put a name to some of the unfamiliar species seen *en route*. I have found this very helpful in identifying unfamiliar insects, reptiles and flowers, in particular.

HIMALAYAN FLOWERS AND VEGETATION

The dominant factors affecting the vegetation of the Himalayas are altitude, climate, and, by virtue of what he has destroyed, man. Lesser factors include slope and aspect, and the underlying geology, though this last is of relatively little importance, which comes as a surprise to those used to botanizing in European mountains, where any outcrop of limestone is a mecca.

The dominant climatic factor is, of course, the monsoon. We have already seen (Chapter 2) how much more important the monsoon is in the eastern and central Himalayas, and this is reflected in the vegetation. At the same time, the eastern and central Himalayas are significantly further south, so that there is much more of a subtropical element in the lower flora, and the altitude zones are shifted slightly upwards. The drier summers of the western Himalayas produce a much less luxurious vegetation, and in the extreme west, in Afghanistan, there is

virtually no forest at all through a combination of drought and grazing animals. Similarly, the vegetation north of the range, in the rain shadow, takes on more of a semi-desert appearance, dominated by scattered dry spiny shrubs rather than trees.

The eastern Himalayan forests

For the purpose of this section, we are looking at the vegetation of the southern slopes of the Himalayas from Uttar Pradesh, eastwards through Nepal to the eastern end of the range. As you go westwards and northwards, towards Kashmir, there is no sudden boundary, but more of a gradual change, so many central areas around Uttar Pradesh have a mixture of eastern and western vegetation.

From the lowest mountain levels up to about 2000 m (6500 ft), the natural vegetation is dominated by subtropical forest, or 'middle

33. Yaks, and yak-cattle hybrids such as this, are an unusual sight for most visitors. Wild yaks, though still present in small numbers, are very unlikely to be seen.

monsoon forest'. This is also a zone of intense cultivation in many parts of the Himalayas, and a very high proportion of this forest has disappeared, though in Bhutan around 60 per cent of it still remains. The forests are very varied, with a wide range of trees and shrubs, often without any one appearing to dominate. There is also a high proportion of evergreens, and the species involved are largely unfamiliar to the eyes of visitors from temperate parts of the world. Common dominants include *Schima, Castanopsis* and laurels.

Upwards from this, at starting heights varying from about 1500 m (5000 ft) in the west of this section, to 2000 m (6500 ft) in the east, the

2　The magnificent view onto the Khumbu glacier
and Pumori, close to Everest, Nepal

1　A colourful mixture of Tibetan-style handicrafts in
a village on a main trek route, Chandrakot, Nepal
(previous page)

3　Nepalese girls in action on a bamboo swing, put up
for the festival of Dasain in autumn

4 *The valley of Hunza, looking north*

5 *A Hunza man, on the trail*

6 *Lamayuru Gompa (monastery), the oldest in Ladakh, built in* AD1177

7 *Vegetable boat visiting house boats on Lake Dal,
Kashmir*

8 *Engraved Buddhas on Mani wall at Gompa
Rangchen, Zanskar*

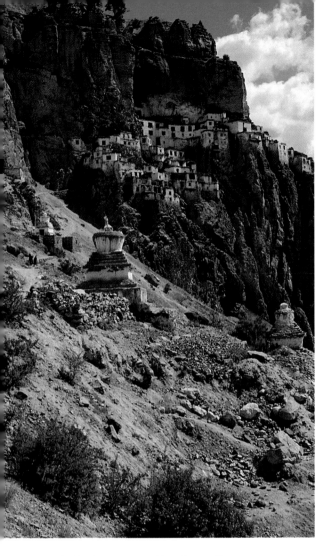

9 *Phuktal monastery, Zanskar valley*

10 *Madhyamakeshwar temple, at 3497m (11,474ft)*
in the Kedarnath Sanctuary, Indian Himalayas

vegetation begins to be of a temperate type, much more familiar to the eyes of Europeans and North Americans. This is the zone of the oaks and rhododendrons. Oaks are abundant throughout this section of the Himalayas at middle altitudes, and there are about ten different species involved, including *Quercus glauca*, *Q. lamellosa*, and *Q. semecarpifolia* (there are no general English names). The oaks differ from many non-Asian species in that they are all evergreen and generally form less impressive trees than their European counterparts, though the Himalayan oak forests are still magnificent places to be in.

The oak forests tend to be more open and accessible than the lower subtropical forests, and they are easier to walk through. They are a prime area for *Rhododendrons*, of which there are about 30 different species in the Himalayas,

mainly in the east. These include the striking and impressive tree rhododendron (*R. arboreum*), that may grow into a tree some 15 m (50 ft) tall, and occurs up to altitudes of 3600 m (12,000 ft). It is widespread almost throughout the Himalayas, especially so in Nepal where it has been adopted as the National Tree. It has the strange habit of producing darker red flowers at lower altitudes, progressively lightening to white at the highest altitudes. Other widespread species of rhododendron in the forests include *R. barbatum*, with bright red flowers and distinctive bristly leaf stalks; and *R. campanulatum*, with paler pink bell-shaped flowers and leaves that are woolly underneath.

34. Rhododendrons flower in spring, before the monsoon, in vast numbers. This is the common tree rhododendron.

These oak forests also support many other plants of interest, including numerous orchids, both epiphytic (on trees) and terrestrial, together with shrubs such as the various fragrant *Daphne* species (familiar in Western gardens, as very early flowering shrubs), and many herbs and climbers. The orchids include examples of *Pleiones, Dendrobiums, Coelogynes, Vandas, Bulbophyllums*, and *Cymbidiums*, which are all epiphytic, and terrestrial species such as the helleborines (*Cephelanthera* and *Epipactis*), the lady's slipper orchids (*Cypripedium*), creeping ladies' tresses (*Goodyera repens*)—a very widespread species that also occurs in Scottish pinewoods—and various other species.

Other plants of interest in this zone that may flower in the trekking seasons include species of *Clematis* such as *C. montana*, familiar in gardens, various *Primulas*, especially in wetter places and clearings, and numerous others.

Generally speaking, the oak forests peter out upwards into coniferous forests of various types, though there is no clear-cut line, and many examples of coniferous woods occur at lower altitudes. In this eastern section, the commonest forest-forming conifers are pines, hemlock, silver fir and larch, especially further east, with cedar and spruce more common in the western parts. The coniferous forests can be exceptionally fine, and an ancient silver fir forest (e.g. *Abies spectabilis*), for example, is cathedral-like in its structure, where it has been left undisturbed.

The commonest pines in the east and centre are the Chir pine (*Pinus roxburghii*), which forms extensive forests, usually at lower altitudes, and the Himalayan blue pine (*P. wallichiana*), which occurs in dry places to a considerable altitude. The Himalayan hemlock (*Tsuga dumosa*) is a beautiful forest-forming tree, occurring throughout the area, as does the silver fir. The deciduous larches, particularly *Larix griffithiana* may form forests from central Nepal eastwards, though they are not abundant. The Himalayan, or Deodar cedar (*Cedrus deo-*

dara)—a familiar garden tree—is primarily a species of the western Himalayas, extending as far west as Afghanistan, though it just creeps into west Nepal.

Usually, the highest limits of tree growth—though often they can be barely classed as trees—are occupied by the birches and the junipers. *Betula utilis*, with distinctly silvery bark, and often decorated with hanging lichens, forms forests right throughout the area, up to a height of well over 4000 m (13,000 ft). These slow-growing forests are being rapidly eroded by the recent demands for building and firewood often associated with the trekking industry. Their rate of growth in the cold, high-altitude climate cannot match the rate of exploitation, so their area is declining, even in protected areas. They are prime habitat and shelter for some of the specialized high-altitude birds and mammals, so the effects of their loss are far-reaching.

The western Himalayan forests

Generally speaking, the forests of the western Himalayas are less extensive, less varied and less important than those of the eastern Himalayas.

The subtropical forest is greatly reduced in extent, going no higher than about 1400 m (4500 ft), and barely occurring at all in the far west. It also tends to be much less rich in species than the eastern forests. The temperate zone is broadly similar, with scattered oak forests, though the number and variety of rhododendrons is greatly reduced; of the woodland species of rhododendron, only *R. campanulatum, R. arboreum*, and *R. lepidotum* extend as far as Kashmir.

There is the same broad pattern of coniferous forests above the oak forests, though different species predominate. For example, the Himalayan, or Deodar cedar is widespread throughout the west, sometimes forming extensive and

35. Piptanthus nepalensis. *A close relative of the laburnum. The golden yellow flowers of this shrub brighten up the mountain woods in spring when few other plants are flowering.*

impressive forests, with individual trees up to 80 m (260 ft), though it is often heavily exploited for timber, or cleared to make new agricultural land. Spruces, silver fir and pine are also present, and may form forests. Birches and junipers again predominate at the highest levels, with the widespread birch *Betula utilis* common, as well as the rather similar *B. jacquemontii*.

ABOVE THE TREE LINE

The highest parts of the Himalayas extend way, way above the natural limits of tree growth, and well beyond the limits of any plant growth. In the eastern Himalayas, the tree line lies at about 4000 m (13,000 ft), varying according to aspect and other local factors, while the further west you go, the lower the tree line is. In the extreme west of the range, it is closer to 3500 m (11,500 ft). Above the tree line, and below the limits of plant growth, lies an area of tremendous interest for the botanist, with a wonderful range of highly-attractive and colourful flowers, including many of considerable medicinal importance. However, the harsh winters and short summers experienced by these high-altitude areas confines the peak of flowering to a relatively short period in midsummer; in the west, this presents no particular problems for the visitor, but in the east—which has a far richer and more spectacular high-altitude flora—the peak flowering coincides with the latter part of the monsoon. Sadly, therefore, few visitors see this spectacular richness, unless special effort is made, for no regular organized tours brave the monsoon.

The highest limits reached by the flowering plants are well above the height that most people will reach, with *Stellaria decumbens* (a stitchwort) and *Arenaria bryophylla* (a sandwort, in the same family) both recorded in Nepal at over 6100 m (20,000 ft)! A few non-flowering plants, such as lichens, are known even beyond this. Generally, the flora becomes pretty sparse and limited at about 5000 m (16,400 ft), though some interesting plants, like the strange cottony,

snowball-like *Saussurea gossypiphora*, are commonest at around this height.

In the monsoonal parts of the Himalayas, it is still possible to see something of the high-altitude flora whilst avoiding the worst of the monsoon. A visit in May will certainly allow the visitor to see a good range of *Primula* species (especially further east), such as *P. aureata*, *P. denticulata*, *P. atrodentata*, *P. deuteronana*, *P. petiolaris*, *P. edgeworthii*, and *P. gracilipes*. At this stage, there may also be some early gentians, the attractive celandine-like *Oxygraphis polypetala*, and early irises such as *I. kumaonensis*. A visit as close to the end of the monsoon as possible can be a reasonable compromise between showers and leeches and a range of monsoon alpine flowers, and there are special autumn-flowering species like the beautiful trumpet gentians, *Gentiana depressa* and *G. ornata*.

Further west, from Afghanistan to Kashmir, and in the north-west trans-Himalayan areas, the summer is the obvious time to visit for high-altitude flowers, coinciding with the peak holiday season.

May is an attractive time here for the lower flowers, especially some of the shrubs, and by June the hay meadows in places like Kashmir are alive with colour. The high-altitude flowers, however, do not really start until July, extending on into August, and a visit in mid-July would probably give the best range of high-altitude specialities, though by this time many of the lower areas are dry and brown. The trans-Himalayan areas are also at their best in July, though generally the flora of these areas is less rich than that of the damper south slopes. Similarly, for anyone who can get there, the flora of the Afghan mountains is best seen in July, with particular specialities like the beautiful cushion *Dionysias* and the lovely *Paraquilegia* to be found.

For anyone visiting the Himalayas to look at flowers, the book *Flowers of the Himalaya*, by Polunin and Stainton (see Bibliography) can be highly recommended; it describes and illustrates a wide range of flowers, and gives some good information on where to go and when. It can be bought in India and Nepal, usually more cheaply than in Britain, though it is not a light book to carry around.

BIRD LIFE IN THE HIMALAYAS

The bird life of the Himalayan area is rich, varied and exciting, and a surprising number of individuals and tours visit the Himalayas purely for the purpose of birdwatching. They are generally well-served with field guides and background books, including *Birds of Nepal* by Fleming *et al.*, *Indian Hill Birds* by Salim Ali, and others (see Bibliography). They do not quite reach the standard of the plethora of European and North American guides, but they are very useful.

It is not possible to do justice to the full range of bird life to be seen in the Himalayas. Nepal alone has recorded over 800 species, for example, and the range extends from lammergeiers, griffon vultures and demoiselle cranes, through numerous species of pheasant, to small and inconspicuous birds like the wren babblers, warblers and tits. For the average walker or general naturalist, though, only a relatively small proportion of this rich avifauna will

36. *The common mynah is the Lowland Nepalese equivalent of the English starling. It is ubiquitous in towns and villages, constantly making its presence felt with calls and screeches.*

become apparent, as so many species are detected only by their calls, or not seen or heard at all! Thus, it is relatively easy to get to grips with the commoner and regularly-seen species.

To give an idea of some of the species involved in commonly-occurring situations, and to whet the appetite, the birds of several such places are briefly described.

The Kathmandu valley has a fortunate mixture of sub-tropical and temperate birds, which is roughly repeated in similar situations along the range, as in Darjeeling and even Srinagar. Over 400 species have been recorded in the valley, with over 200 recorded on a single Christmas-Day count! For the newly-arrived visitor, hotel windows and flat roofs provide excellent viewpoints for seeing the fliers.

Black kites are everywhere, while vultures, buzzards, eagles and occasional harriers soar overhead on the thermals, often beyond the range of the naked eye. Swallows, martins and swifts streak around, manoeuvring between houses and temples without difficulty, while bright white egrets ply back and forth from their colonies to the riversides and wet fields. Striated swallows in particular, recognizable by their reddish rumps, nest inside many houses, benefiting from the lack of glass in the windows, the general shortage of cats, and the tolerance of the owners. Cattle egrets, strongly marked with orange-brown in the breeding season, fill whole trees with their noisy colonies. A pair of spotted doves, with their characteristic speckled collars, may fly quickly past to settle in a tree. A loud burst of song heralds the arrival of a jaunty little black and white bird known as the magpie robin, or robin dayal. This aptly-named bird is common around Kathmandu, and has an annoying habit of starting to sing outside the window

37. The ubiquitous house crow on a rooftop in Kathmandu.

at about 4.30 a.m.!

The common mynah is a brown, starling-like bird with a yellowish eye patch, and is always in evidence scavenging, screeching and jostling, eating almost anything. Another abundant bird of city life is the house crow, black but with a grey nape and breast, and very cheeky and tame. Smallish green birds, with a strange tuft of hairs at the base of the beak, are barbets of various species, found wherever there are woods or scattered trees.

A walk out to the edge of town, or along a riverbank, will quickly turn up more species, depending on the time of year. Drongos are common in lower areas, especially black drongos; they are elegant black birds with long forked tails and a habit of perching on wires, from where they chase insects. Along the wetter parts of the riverbanks there are waders in plenty, varying according to season, including many that will be familiar to Europeans, such as common and green sandpipers, redshank and little stint. In wooded or scrubby areas, cuckoos are common, especially the Eurasian cuckoo ('cuck-oo') and the Indian cuckoo (a melodic four-note 'one more bot-tle'). Golden orioles warble away, hidden in the depths of the trees, while a small dark crested bird with red below the tail and a long chattering song is the red-vented bulbul.

By contrast, the birds of a typical high-altitude, mid-Himalayan village are very different, and much fewer, though full of interest. The all-black, raven-like jungle crow is very common in higher-altitude villages, and in the clearings around them, perching on roofs and trees to watch for carrion and refuse. The larger and shaggier raven is less common and generally less tame, though it may come very close to houses at

38. A heraldic-looking cuckoo uses a tree stripped for cattle fodder as a vantage point.

times. (When living in a house in Langtang village (central Nepal, 3300 m or 10,800 ft), I watched our Bhotia neighbours putting out some red figures on a log by the window, which at first I thought were made of wax. Within a few minutes, a raven appeared and ate its way through the lot, sending jungle crows packing if they tried to take part in the feast. I found out later that the figures were made from barley meal coloured with red dye, and they were clearly highly attractive to birds.)

The choughs are close relatives of the crows, and two species occur at high altitude in Nepal: the red-billed chough and the alpine, or yellow-billed, chough. Both are black with red legs, but they have different coloured curving beaks, and slightly different habits, though mixed flocks may occur. The pale, almost silvery, snow pigeon may feed in large flocks in the fields around the highest villages, leaving at dusk to go and roost on high ledges, even above the snowline, for safety from predators. Bearded vultures, or lammergeiers, are huge birds with a wingspan of over 2.5 m (8 ft), a diamond-shaped tail and a golden head; and they are often seen gliding gracefully along a hillside, or even visiting the village refuse area. The Himalayan griffon vulture is a much heavier, darker bird, 'like a tea-tray in the sky', which is quite common in the mountains, and golden eagles are not infrequent, though you have to keep watching the skies for them.

On forest edges near villages, and deeper into the forests, one of Nepal's most spectacular birds can be found—the extraordinary Impeyan pheasant, or Danphe bird. This striking large blue, green and orange bird, with a turquoise crest (on the male), is Nepal's national bird, though it occurs throughout the Himalayas. If a male

39. In Bhutan, the amount of forest cover, and the area of wilderness, is much greater than in other Himalayan countries, resulting in a very rich wildlife. Drukgyel Dzong (in ruins) and Chomolhari.

breaks cover near you, you are likely to notice it, as it usually emerges with a noisy cackle and glides off down the hillside calling loudly. Unfortunately for it, it is too heavy in relation to its wing size to fly back up, so it will have to walk to regain its original vantage point! Close relatives of the Danphe, though less often seen, include the blood pheasant, the Kalij pheasant, and the snow partridge and Tibetan snowcock, the last two of which may be found around the snowline and close to several mountaineering base camps.

Along the rivers there are some conspicuous birds to be seen. Plumbeous redstarts are very common and tame, recognizable by the dark, slatey blue male, which has a red tail, and the white-rumped female. Equally common and distinctive are the white-capped riverchats, with red tails, blue-black bodies and a white cap on the head. Another river-dweller, though much less common, is the striking ibisbill—a large greyish wader, with a bright red, downwardly curving beak, adapted for prising invertebrates out from under stones. It breeds in the high glacial valleys of the Himalayas above 3500 m (11,500 ft), moving downwards in winter.

In addition to the residents and breeders, many of the high valleys are migration routes, and many species will settle for a while, or be seen overhead. Poor weather will often force birds down into the valleys before they have reached their destination, such as the demoiselle crane seen at 4200 m (13,800 ft) near Mount Everest.

MAMMALS AND REPTILES IN THE HIMALAYAS

The Himalayas offer no spectacle such as the mammals of the African plains, nor even the rich fauna of many lowland Indian game reserves, yet the mammalian fauna is rich and varied overall. Few people are likely to visit the Himalayas purely for mammal-watching, let alone watch for long, as they are generally difficult to see at all, and many people walk for several weeks in the mountains without seeing a mammal. Books on mammals are also rather less good than for birds or flowers, though Prater's *Book of Indian Mammals* is useful. Altogether, the range of mammals is very wide, from snow leopards and bears, through flying squirrels, to mice and voles, but you do have to work hard to see most of them. As a general rule, it pays to get up very early and be out on the trail by dawn to give yourself the best chance of seeing mammals; most of them keep well away from well-trodden trails during the day. Evenings can also be fruitful, but the main part of the day, when most people are out and about, is the least productive.

The mammals most frequently seen in the mountains are almost certainly the beautiful Langur monkeys, with their grey and white fur, and black faces. They occur in family troupes, of between 10 and 20 animals, with a strict social organization, and may be seen moving through the trees or amongst rocks with amazing agility, right up to the limits of the tree line. Watching a female carrying a baby as she swings from tree to tree, or leaps many metres between rocks, is a sight worth seeing.

Another reasonably commonly seen mammal is the Himalayan squirrel, which inhabits forest areas from 2–3000 m (6500–9850 ft). Flying squirrels tend to be more nocturnal, but occasionally one may get an unexpected view of one as it sails from tree to tree, or down to the ground. They are only gliding, or parachuting, but have been known to travel 100 m (328 ft) in a leap, and have great ability to land softly.

A selection of other mammals and reptiles that the average walker might expect to see is as follows:

Rhesus macaque monkeys are abundant around many towns and larger villages, especially where there are temples. They are given a fair amount of protection and tolerance, despite their raids on crops, and are sometimes called 'temple monkeys' because of their association with religious places. Higher in the Himalayas, they are rarer, and noticeably furrier to cope with the cold winters.

Tigers are more widespread in the lowlands and the foothills, with well-known reserves in India and Nepal carrying good populations, but they also occur well up into the Himalayas, at low densities, and have been recorded as high as 3050 m (10,000 ft).

Common leopards are not specifically mountain animals, though they occur well up into the Himalayas, both in forests and in more open country. The snow leopard is very specifically a mountain animal, and it occurs at extremely low densities right throughout the range at altitudes of from 3000 to 4500 m (9850 to 14,800 ft), usually above the tree line. Its main prey is the blue sheep (see p 76), and it is most likely to be seen in association with flocks of these in very remote areas. Sadly, it is still being hunted, despite bans on the sale of its pelt. The clouded leopard is a little-known species that occurs throughout the eastern Himalayas.

Other cats include the jungle cat, the leopard cat and the beautiful lynx.

Wolves occur in the drier, more open parts of the western Himalayas, becoming quite common in places, especially in Afghanistan. They gather into packs in winter, but in summer they are generally solitary, and found at high altitudes. I met one outside my tent at 3500 m (11,500 ft) above the Salang Pass in Afghanistan, in July. Other Himalayan members of the dog family include jackals, which are quite common around hill towns and on up to well over 3500 m (11,500 ft) in places; the red fox, which is almost ubiquitous; and the Indian wild dog, which is most likely to be seen in trans-Himalayan regions.

Bears occur widely throughout the Himalayas, though not abundantly. The Himalayan black bear, with its distinctive black fur and white 'V' across the chest, occurs throughout the forested areas of the Himalayas, usually staying below the tree line. The brown bear tends to occur in more open areas, often above the tree line, mainly in the western Himalayas and Bhutan. The black bear is more likely to be encountered by the walker, and, since it is the more aggressive of the two, it is best avoided.

Giant pandas do not occur within the Himalayas, but their close relative the red panda is reasonably frequent in higher forests from Nepal eastwards. Though primarily nocturnal, sleeping in trees during the day, it is met by people surprisingly often.

Among the more likely animals that the Himalayan traveller will meet are some of the weasel family, especially the beech marten, the yellow-throated marten and the Himalayan weasel. All are reasonably common in upper forests, and may hunt in the day.

Bats are regularly seen at dusk, in all sorts of habitats, up to surprisingly high altitudes. The commonest species in the Himalayas are probably the greater eastern horseshoe bat, the serotine, and the Indian pipistrelle. Fruit bats, or flying foxes, occur in the Kathmandu valley in noisy tree colonies, but not up into the Himalayas proper.

The Indian porcupine is reasonably common in high, drier areas in the west, preferring rocky unforested hillsides. Although individuals are not often seen, they frequently leave quills as evidence of their presence.

For the high-altitude walker, one of the commonest and most welcome sights is the Himalayan mouse hare, or pika. These small, guinea-pig-like animals may be abundant above the tree line throughout the Himalayas, and though nervous, they are usually inquisitive enough to reappear quickly if you stop and wait a few minutes. Marmots, by contrast, are rather infrequent.

Yaks are regularly seen in their domestic form, and they are as fascinating as a wild animal to most people since they are so different to anything else. Domestic yaks come in a wide range of patterns, most commonly black and white, but they are regularly hybridized with cattle to produce various offspring such as *dzopkios* with particular combinations of characteristics. They are incredibly hardy animals, found only at the highest altitudes, where they are used as beasts of burden, for milk, and for meat, wool and leather. The original wild yak does still survive, though very rare, mainly in the highest and driest areas such as Ladakh, Dolpo and elsewhere. It is more likely to be even-coloured blackish-brown, without white, and especially shaggy, though it is difficult to separate particular lone domestic yaks from genuine wild ones.

Various wild goats and sheep, or related animals, occur in the highest parts of the Himalayas, though it is often difficult to get close enough to them to be able to identify them with certainty. The blue sheep (previously mentioned as the prey of the snow leopard), which is as much a goat as a sheep, lives in herds in trans-Himalayan areas all along the range; the ibex is a western Himalayan species; the markhor is also a western species, from Kashmir to Afghanistan, distinguishable by the striking twisted horns of the male. The Himalayan tahr is much more widespread, living at high altitudes almost throughout the Himalayas, though it is unlikely to be seen by the casual observer—you need to scan the cliffs with binoculars regularly. They are highly agile, but occasionally make mistakes—one fell off the huge cliff that towered above the house I lived in at Langtang, and landed just in front of the house, dead. It was probably an old individual. There are also two 'goat antelopes', that are something of a mixture, as their name implies. Both the serow and the goral live in rocky but generally wooded areas throughout the range. They are most likely to be seen leaving open, grassy areas in the early morning, or coming out of the forest in the late evening.

Finally, there are several deer that occur in the Himalayas. The Kashmir stag or hangul is probably the most impressive. It is a form of the more widespread red deer, occurring only in Kashmir, especially in the Dachigam reserve. Muntjac, or barking deer, are small mainly nocturnal deer, most often detected by their dog-like bark, or their alarm call (a series of higher-pitched barks) when disturbed. Musk deer are incredibly secretive, and most unlikely to be seen—a biologist who researched them for several years only saw deer for a total of 15 minutes in his first year-and-a-quarter in the field, in one of their strongholds! They are hunted mercilessly for their musk pods which are sold at incredibly high prices as aphrodisiacs, and they have become increasingly rare, even in protected areas.

The Yeti, or Abominable Snowman

There is one animal that visitors to the high Himalayas hope to see more than any other, though none of them are really successful, and that is the famous yeti. Myths, legends, third-hand stories and near-misses abound, yet despite expeditions specifically to find it, and thousands of people on the lookout for it, there is really no hard evidence that it exists.

But the possibility lingers on. Local people are adamant that it exists, occasional unexplained footprints *do* turn up, and the territory that it is said to occupy is vast and difficult. The golden langur of Assam was unknown to science until 1955; so its discovery would be by no means impossible. If it does exist, it seems most likely that the population, which is probably very small and scattered, lives primarily north of the Himalayas, where there are few residents and virtually no visitors, and occasionally it strays onto the southern slopes.

The controversy will not be settled until one is found and captured, or photographed at close range, and this may be some time away yet. Incidentally, the 'yeti scalp' at Dingboche monastery near Everest is a well-known fake, made up from bits of other animals!

CHAPTER SEVEN

Trekking in the Himalayas: background information

In the Himalayan region, the word 'trekking' has become standard for any type of walking in the mountains involving staying away from base for more than a day or so. It is one of the most incredible experiences that the world has to offer, assuming that you choose a suitable trek at a suitable time of year, and I can unhesitatingly recommend it to anyone who is visiting the area. The Himalayas take on a completely new meaning and aspect as soon as you start walking, even if you are only on an easy route with an organized group—you see much more of the local people, going about their lives largely unaffected by the Western world, you appreciate their problems as you struggle up the hills, you see some of the most spectacular views in the world, and you come closer to a wonderful range of birds and other animals, flowers, butterflies, and other forms of natural life. It can also be extremely satisfying to have made a physically demanding journey, possibly to high altitude, and felt yourself get fitter each day (after the effects of the first few days wear off!).

This chapter is intended as a background guide to how to prepare for a trek, what to expect from it, how to plan or select one, and how to cope once you are on it.

HOW TO GO

There are basically two ways you can tackle a trek in the Himalayas: by going with an organized group or by going it alone. Each has its advantages and disadvantages, though most people will opt for the organized group on their first visit, even though they may try organizing their own trek on a subsequent trip.

Organized treks

The very words 'organized' or 'group' may be anathema to many potential walkers seeking to experience the wilderness of the Himalayas, whilst to others it represents the only way they would wish to travel. In fact, organized trips can suit most types of people, and they are an excellent way to see the Himalayas—a far cry from the typical 'group' travel of cruises or up-market archaeological tours, for example.

There is an abundance of tour companies specializing in trips to the Himalayas, and any Sunday paper, adventure magazine or natural history magazine will carry advertisements for them (see p 137). Some offer a very wide range of tours, covering all the countries in the Himalayas (except Afghanistan, at present), with special-interest versions looking at, for example, natural history, and a range of grades from very easy to very difficult. Other operators include just a few treks, often as part of an India tour, or a more general holiday in Nepal. You are bound to be able to find what you want, though the problem is more likely to lie in deciding what you *do* want!

You may already have a predetermined idea of where you wish to go, which makes life easier (though when you receive the brochures and

realize the range of possibilities, you may then find the decision more difficult). If you have no particular ideas, the first essentials are to consider your level of fitness (or potential fitness, by the time you come to go) and the amount of time you have. Some of the treks to more remote areas inevitably take three weeks or more, and if you do not have this time, they have to be ruled out. Some treks will involve crossing high passes, perhaps some ice and snow work, and possibly some long days of walking, and all brochures should give an idea of the degree of difficulty, by a grading system, with respect to each trek; think hard about whether you can manage a given trek, as it can be disastrous both for you and the rest of the group if you find you cannot continue after you have started.

Apart from these two basic considerations, your choice will probably be determined by whether your special interests are catered for, whether you have heard of any particular area mentioned, the cost, and other factors, which might even include how nice the accompanying pictures in the brochure were! One general piece of advice is to avoid trips that try to do too much; although it is tempting to try to pack a lot in, experience suggests that people who go on tours which include a few Indian sights, some wildlife reserves, a few days in Kathmandu, a quick trek, and then some river rafting, for example, are rarely satisfied. Personally, too, I have always found that a visit with a trek of at least two weeks, reaching some really remote and exciting country, has always proved most satisfying. You can always hope to come back to try some of the other things—most people do!

On the trail with a group

Trekking with an organized group in the Himalayas is the nearest thing to luxury that you can expect while walking in wilderness mountains, especially with the well-organized companies operating in Nepal. Just about everything is done for you with the exception of the actual walking—and usually done very well, too. You are supported by a considerable team, consisting normally of a leader, a group of Sherpas with a head Sherpa (Sirdar), and a mass of porters, as many as needed. The porters, who are usually of the Thamang race in Nepal, carry about 27–29.5 kg (60–65 lb) each, which will be made up of all the camping and cooking gear, the participants' personal luggage, together with food, medical kit and miscellaneous items. As a participant, you do not need to carry anything at all if you do not wish to, but in practice, most people carry a small rucksack containing washing things, pull-over, camera etc., leaving the bulk for the porters.

In the morning, you are woken at dawn (usually about 06.00) with a cup of tea, and some warm washing water. Breakfast, which can be quite substantial, is ready in half an hour or so—porridge, eggs, toast and coffee are all on the menu. Afterwards, you only need to wash or whatever you want to do, pack up your things for the day, and that's it; all the washing up, striking of camp, etc., is done by the Sherpa/ kitchen team, and the Sherpas also organize all the loading up of porters. The porters sleep in local villages, or out in the open under a blanket, and organize their own food. They fade away into the darkness in the evening, and reappear out of the gloom in the morning, ready for work.

When you set off, some Sherpas will set off with you, to help any who are slower, liaise with the leader over the route, and generally be on hand. Others will complete the packing up of the kitchen and camp, and set off later, overtaking you somewhere along the way, in time to arrive at a suitable lunch spot, make a fire, and get lunch cooking. You then have a couple of hours over lunch, to catch up with your diary, do some washing, take photos, or go to sleep in the sun, before moving off for a relatively short afternoon

40. *The villages of Khumjung and Khunde, in the high Khumbu region around Everest. There is nowhere in the world in which you have to be more careful about altitude problems.*

walk, stopping at about 16.00 if there is a suitable campsite. The cooking staff will again pack up and move off, ready to get organized for cooking the evening meal. When the porters arrive, which may be before or after you, the tents can be unpacked and set up by the Sherpas, and the whole camp made ready.

Whilst actually walking, there is ample scope for people to go at their own speed, or stop for anything, and in a well-organized group there will always be a Sherpa at the rear to make sure no-one gets lost. On the first trip I ever led, to Everest Base Camp, one participant had never before walked anywhere, and was several stone overweight. For at least the first week, he would arrive for lunch, worn out, just as the rest were ready to leave, and would arrive at each camp after dark, which obviously involved a fair amount of Sherpas' and leader's time in just ensuring that he arrived and did not disappear on the wrong route! Strangely enough, in the end, he was one of only about six, from a group of fifteen, who made it right to Base Camp, at over 5500 m (18,000 ft), so it shows what can be done with persistence.

So, walking with a group can be a relatively easy way to tackle the mountains, without any worry over carrying a heavy weight, finding somewhere to stay, keeping to the route, or getting enough to eat, and it can be a pleasantly sociable experience if the group members work well together or have similar interests. By contrast, though, you have to adhere to a fairly fixed itinerary, you have less contact with local people, and less feeling of adventure and independence; so it depends on what you want and what you can manage.

Going it alone

The alternative to booking up with a group and going on a fixed tour lies in going it alone. In fact,

41. Kitchen porters, with a trekking group, toiling up a mountain trail on their way to set up a lunch-stop.

there are two ways of doing this, which are distinctly different: either by backpacking, carrying all your own stuff and being completely independent; or by going through a local agent and hiring your own cooking/leading/carrying staff, or even going directly to the people themselves, though this is much more difficult and unsatisfactory.

Backpacking is something that people either love or hate; some people are simply unable to carry a heavy load, whilst others feel too constrained by it anyway; yet some people feel a total sense of freedom in carrying all their own gear and going exactly when and where they choose. It does demand a little more thought and preparation than the other forms of trekking, since you not only have to be walking-fit, but fit enough to walk carrying a heavy pack without getting too tired to enjoy it, and without sustaining injury as a result. For example, you are much more likely to inflame leg joints when carrying a heavy load if you are unused to it, especially on one of the many steep downhill descents. Your original packing has to be thorough and careful, since you have to make sure you will have all you might need; yet it must also weigh as little as possible, though of course much depends on your load-carrying ability, and the quality and size of your rucksack.

You can either take a lightweight tent and cooking utensils, or choose to stay in local lodges or houses, or a combination of the two—e.g. sleeping in your tent, but eating in lodges or tea-houses along the route. The decision will partly depend on where you are going—if you are staying high for a while, or going somewhere particularly remote, then you will simply not find anywhere to sleep or eat. This particularly applies to the high parts of the Karakoram and western Himalayas, especially in Pakistan, where people may be few and far between and often unwelcoming. This sort of trip, therefore, involves more attention to the route and the gleaning of as much information as possible in advance.

42. Naudanda, near Annapurna. Popular areas such as this have a wealth of accommodation, of varying quality, which makes it easier to trek on your own.

43. In extreme circumstances, it is possible to sleep in summer grazing huts at high altitude. They should be treated with great respect and not damaged in any way.

If you follow the second option, and organize your staff yourself, you will probably (though not necessarily) save money, compared to an organized group, and you will find yourself subject to some of the same constraints. You may find it difficult to persuade your staff to depart from their traditional stopping points, which makes it more difficult for you to vary your day length according to your requirements; there is some sense in this, since the porters cannot walk much further than the standard day, and they have to find a convenient village to sleep in; and there needs to be water and a flat area to stop on. Thus your flexibility is somewhat reduced once you take on staff, but you can still decide, for example, to stay several days at a pleasant place, or make a detour up an interesting side-valley, which you cannot do with a group. It may also be straightforward enough to lengthen your trip if you decide there is more to see, though again you may find that your staff are already committed to the next trip and cannot stay as long as you would like.

Backpacking is the most flexible approach in terms of itinerary and timing.

WHAT TO TAKE

It would not be appropriate to itemize a standard list for a trek, since conditions vary so much; for example, the difference between a seven-day trek on the southern slopes of Annapurna in November, and a three to four-week trip up into the high northern Karakoram is extreme. However, there are some general points that are likely to apply to most trips to any altitude.

Footwear is clearly of paramount importance, though there is a fair amount of unnecessary 'mystique' talked about it. The critical points are that your footwear remains comfortable despite being used all day and every day, and that it will last the duration of the trip. Whatever you intend to wear, you should try them out thoroughly in conditions that involve both uphill and downhill walking, to see that they suit you. Sandals and flip-flops are likely to be very unsuitable, but reasonably strong trainers are fine for most walks. If you expect to cross snow or ice, you need to be prepared accordingly. A pair of spare comfortable shoes for use in the evenings are useful, especially if they could be walked in, in an emergency.

Socks are important, too, and you will need several pairs. Nylon socks are much worse than woollen or wool mixture, and it is useful to have at least one thick pair. If you are not a regular walker, it is quite likely that you will get blisters, and a supply of plasters would undoubtedly be useful.

The sun at higher altitudes is particularly intense and able to burn, since it has passed through less atmosphere, and you are very liable to suffer from sunburn. A strong protective cream, especially for the face, is very important, and if you are prone to burning, a total blocker is best. Lips tend to dry easily in this atmosphere, especially as you keep your mouth open more than usual because of all that uphill walking, and some form of lip cream is very useful. A hat is an excellent idea, especially for bald or balding males, who may suffer unduly without one. Sunglasses are helpful if you wear them nor-

44. Porters on the Lower Trisuli valley trail, central Nepal.

mally, or if you are going to high altitudes or snowy areas, where the light can be very intense.

Clothing is obviously important, but requirements vary enormously. For a lowish level trek (up to about 3000 m or 9850 ft) in a main trekking period, you can expect very warm days, cool evenings, and cold nights, but not seriously cold. Therefore you need to be able to wear various layers, from shorts and tee-shirt for walking, up to several layers in the evening. If you go in for getting up before dawn to climb a nearby viewpoint, you will find it extremely cold before the sun reaches you—though it is usually more than worth it. If you expect to go much higher, or the season is closer to midwinter, you will be in for some severe cold. Although the days will remain warm if it is sunny, the temperature will drop considerably in cloudier weather. As the sun leaves you on an evening with a clear sky the temperature drops at an incredible rate at high altitudes, and you will be glad of a lot of warm clothing, or numerous layers. A down sleeping bag is essential for most people at great heights.

Rucksacks are a matter of personal preference, but, if backpacking, you must be sure that it is large enough to take all you want, strong enough to withstand a lot of rough use, and comfortable enough to wear all day. If you are going with a group, then a much smaller daysack will suffice, unless, as I do, you persist in carrying large quantities of camera equipment, tripods, and exposed and unexposed film, together with field guides, notebooks and all the normal requirements!

A good group will carry an extensive supply of *medicines and first aid materials*. If you are travelling alone, however, a pack made up with the help of a doctor and/or someone with experience of Himalayan travel is an essential requirement. See section below on keeping well.

Other useful items to take include a good torch *with spare batteries*, some string, an all-purpose knife, scissors if not on the knife, safety pins, some kind of repair outfit strong enough to deal with repairs to shoes and rucksacks, and some matches. Photographic requirements are dealt with separately in Chapter 10.

KEEPING WELL ON TREK

It is essential to keep as well as you can whilst trekking. If you get ill, apart from the fact that it could be serious, your schedule will slip, you may hold up your group, and you will fail to appreciate what you have paid so much to experience.

The first step is to make sure you are as well as possible before you go. Have a medical and dental check-up, and do something about the results. Begin a programme of exercise to make sure you are fit, and consider taking a course of vitamins for at least a month before departure to help boost your immune system and get you to a peak of health. Some injections are essential, as advised by your doctor, and it is wise to start finding out about this some months before you go, if you are likely to need the full range.

Once there, you will almost certainly be open to many more diseases and infections than you are at home, and it is wise to take as many precautions as possible. Overall, eat as well as possible and take a supply of strong, well-balanced vitamins with you, with some extra vitamin C, as there is evidence that this regime, together with low stress and adequate sleep, boosts your immune system.

More specific precautions have to be taken as well, however. The most prevalent problem are water-borne diseases such as the dysenteries and minor 'tummy upsets', any of which can greatly reduce your walking ability. Take water sterilizing tablets (or iodine is better still), and, if possible, boil your water for at least ten minutes in addition. Fruit, or anything similar, should be

45. In more remote parts of the Himalayas the villages are more primitive, and not geared up to accommodate trekkers, so you have to be self-contained.

well washed in sterilizing solution before eating, and this should include fruit which you will peel—it is very easy to transfer the bacteria from skin to flesh as you peel them. Avoid foods which you cannot be sure about, like yoghurt or ice cream, and if you buy tea or coffee in tea-houses, it is best to have it poured directly into your own mug. Take some antiseptic soap and wash your hands regularly to try to keep them free of infective bacteria, which can be picked up almost everywhere.

As a general rule, the longer one stays in the area, the more relaxed you become about these precautions. It is certainly true that you can develop an immunity against the mild stomach disorders—and in any case some people seem to be less affected than others—but you are unlikely to develop immunity to the more serious dysenteries and hepatitis, which can be picked up from the same sources. In principle, therefore, it is wisest to carry on with the precautions, though it can be difficult at times, especially if you eat out.

An array of medicaments can help in some cases, though there are problems. Taking intestinal blockers like Lomotil relieves some symptoms, though it certainly does not help the infection to go away. Taking antibiotics might sound like a good idea, but, in my experience, it usually seems to prolong the problem. You usually do not know what form of infection you are dealing with, or how long to continue the course, and there is a danger of reducing your immunity to the next infection. People who continue to take antibiotics as a sort of prophylactic rarely seem to be fully well, but perhaps they would have been worse still without them. The general advice of seasoned Himalayan travellers is to let all minor ailments take their course, and only act if they are obviously turning into something more serious.

46. The religious sites at Gosainkund lakes, central Nepal, are reached by many thousands of pilgrims every summer, despite the moderate-altitude passes leading into them.

Skin wounds should be washed with antiseptic soap or disinfectant, and kept as clean as possible. They can very easily turn into a more widespread infection which can be quite painful and even debilitating. Antibiotic cream is a useful extra aid.

ALTITUDE PROBLEMS

There is nowhere in the world where you are more likely to suffer from altitude problems than in the Himalayas. Almost any trek takes you into altitude zones where problems may occur, and a good many treks involve altitudes that can give rise to serious problems.

As a general rule, altitude problems can begin at about 3000–3500 m (10,000–11,500 ft), though they are more likely to begin higher up if you have walked steadily up to the higher altitude. People vary considerably in their reaction to altitude, and some people suffer severely and adjust slowly. However, the overriding general rule is to ascend gradually, with an increasing number of night-time stops at higher altitudes. The serious problems almost invariably only occur where the sufferer has flown into high altitude, or has walked into a high altitude area by gaining height too quickly. Once above about 4500 m (14,800 ft), you cannot expect to be able to gain further height quickly until you have acclimatized, and any well-organized group will ensure that this is the case.

You need to be able to recognize the symptoms of altitude sickness, even in its early stages, and be able to turn back. If the symptoms are ignored, altitude sickness can become a killer, through pulmonary or cerebral oedema.

At higher altitudes, the atmospheric pressure is much lower, and the availability of oxygen falls. The earliest and least worrying symptom is simply increased breathlessness when climbing hills; in itself, this is not a great problem. However, if you begin to develop a persistent headache, feel sick, lose your appetite, sleep badly, have an increased output of urine, or generally feel very tired—or any combination of these—you should certainly not go any higher. If you continue to suffer, the only remedy is to lose height, quickly, to the altitude at which you feel well again. If you ignore these symptoms, and climb on upwards, you will be exposing yourself to serious danger.

Finally, although diuretics such as Lasex are helpful in relieving the symptoms of altitude problems, they are not a cure for it. Many people appear to feel that if they have some tablets with them they can safely ignore the problem—this is not the case.

CHAPTER EIGHT

Trekking in the Himalayas: where to go

The possibilities for trekking in the Himalayas are absolutely endless. It would be possible to spend a lifetime roaming the range, and still find more to do. For most people, the problem is not to find yet another place to go, but rather to decide which area will best suit their needs given that they may only have one chance. The odd thing is, though, that when you first go to the Himalayas, you imagine that one trip will be enough, that you will be satisfied by this. Hardly anyone is, and it simply leads to the desire to go somewhere else, to somewhere more remote, or to a similar area at a different season!

If you are trekking alone, your possible treks really are endless, as there is absolutely no reason why you need to stay on the standard routes and circuits; you can stray off into magnificent country, barely visited by foreigners, with relatively little effort. Your only limitation as an independent traveller is Bhutan, where only group travel is encouraged. Even if you travel with an organized group your choice is hardly limited, as the companies specializing in Himalayan travel offer a very wide range of choices, particularly in Nepal, but covering most of the other key areas too.

This chapter is a guide to the main trekking areas in the Himalayas, drawing attention to some of the highlights of each, arranged by country from west to east along the chain, concluding with China (Tibet). It cannot provide a day-by-day itinerary, but rather an overview to help in selection, or just to read about. There is a good range of trekking guides available for most areas, giving more detailed itineraries (see Bibliography).

AFGHANISTAN

Areas: At the time of writing, opportunities for trekking in any shape or form are, to say the least, limited. Afghanistan is one of the most dramatic and exciting countries in the world, and it would be a fascinating place to go trekking in, if and when it opens up. Since the general trend is for closed countries to open more, it is by no means improbable that Afghanistan will eventually re-open to travellers.

Some areas of high mountain country are quite easily accessible, and there are a number of high passes that give easy access to high country. The Salang Pass crosses the range at over 3500 m (11,500 ft), and there is a rough snow-cutters' track that goes on beyond the tunnel for about another 500 m (1640 ft) up, to a beautiful small lake. The pass is on the main route north from Kabul and is readily accessible in normal times. Similarly, the Unai Pass provides access to some fine country further west.

Perhaps the most exciting area of Afghanistan that is not too remote is the border land of Nuristan—the land of light. This lies next to Pakistan and the people include a white-skinned race, sometimes claimed to be descendants of soldiers in Alexander the Great's army.

The ultimate challenge in Afghanistan is the

47. The monastery at Tengboche, in the shadow of Everest, is one of the most popular and attractive trekking locations.

Wakhan corridor—the pan-handle at the north-eastern extremity, where China, the USSR, Pakistan and Afghanistan meet. This is one of the most remote areas of the world, though it used to be visited occasionally by scientific expeditions, and, sadly, by hunters in search of the Marco Polo sheep.

Seasons: Afghanistan is a non-monsoon country, with very cold winters in the north and in the mountains. The possible visiting season therefore extends roughly from April to October, or a little less where high passes are contemplated, as snow can lie late into the first half of summer.

PAKISTAN

Although still much less well-organized than trekking in Nepal, or even in India, the possibilities for trekking in the northern areas of Pakistan

are immense and exciting. It is generally much more difficult country than further east, with fewer villages and a harsher climate, but this is mitigated to some extent by several roads running deep into the area which allow the possibility of short treks in high mountain areas. There are local trekking agencies in Rawalpindi, Islamabad and Gilgit who can assist with preparation and breaking down the formalities, and some trips can be organized through UK and other operators abroad.

Areas: This confused and convoluted area of high mountains and glaciers does not fall readily into divisions. The somewhat arbitrary divisions adopted follow that of the excellent book

Pakistan—a Travel Survival Kit, which covers the trekking routes in more detail than this book can.

Lower northern treks: Around Gilgit and southwards towards the Indian border, there is great potential for a wide range of treks, including a number of easy ones with unrestricted access— i.e. permits and guides are not needed. It also includes some extremely difficult areas, particularly around the massive peak of Nanga Parbat (see panel).

Nanga Parbat is the eighth highest mountain in the world, at 8125 m high (26,657 ft). Its position at the western end of the Great Himalayan Range is isolated from any other mountain of comparable height for a long distance around, so it stands out like a cathedral above houses, dominating the area. It is well-known as a difficult and dangerous mountain to climb, and has caused the deaths of at least 50 climbers since Mummery in 1897. Not surprisingly, it is also an object of considerable superstition and awe amongst the people living under its shadow.

Baltistan: Baltistan is an extensive and beautiful mountain area of the Karakorams, rich in high peaks, glaciers and beautiful valleys. It used to be part of Ladakh, and still has something of a Tibetan feel about it, despite centuries of Muslim rule. It is probably the most important trekking and mountaineering area in Pakistan, primarily due to the presence of K2 (Mount Godwin-Austen), the Siachen glacier, which is the longest in the Himalayas, and a vast area of dramatic mountain scenery.

K2 mountain is the second highest mountain in the world, after Everest (there have been recent claims that it is actually higher than Everest, though the difference is academic as far as the

viewer is concerned), at 8611 m (28,250 ft). It is remote and inaccessible, something like a hundred miles from the nearest road or track, so trekkers or mountaineers have to spend a considerable time in just reaching the base. The name Mount Godwin-Austen is still occasionally used, though it was never officially adopted; it was suggested as a tribute to Colonel Godwin-Austen who carried out the original surveying of its valleys and glaciers, but did not find much favour with authority at the time.

The principal town of the area, though it is nothing special, is Skardu, and a number of treks start off from here. Most treks head north and east towards the high mountains of K2, Masherbrum, Gasherbrum, and the extraordinary Concordia, where several glaciers meet, surrounded by some of the highest mountains in the world. Treks into this area are relatively long and arduous, and not suited to the inexperienced.

Hunza valley and the surrounding area: This is another beautiful and extremely mountainous area. The Hunza valley once held a reputation as a Shangri-La, partly because it was so incredibly remote; it used to be only really accessible from the north and most of its links were with China and Tibet. However, the coming of the Karakoram highway has totally changed that, and affected many of the valley's ancient customs, and it is no longer seen in quite the same way. Indeed, exports from Hunza find their way into health food shops all over the Western world, in the form of particularly wizened dried apricots. The long valley makes a good setting-off point for a number of treks into wild mountainous country with many glaciers.

INDIA

India reaches up to the Himalayas in two widely separated arms, divided by the Kingdom of Nepal. Weather conditions and trekking arrangements are different in each so they are treated separately.

48. Trekking allows you to get much closer to village life than any vehicle-borne form of transport does.

Western Indian Himalayas

Although the western Indian Himalayas are steadily becoming more popular as a trekking destination—deservedly so—they still lag considerably behind Nepal in the facilities offered. For the backpacker, too, there is a marked difference in that it is much more difficult to simply walk from lodge to lodge in the high hills, finding food and accommodation easily—in much of the Indian Himalayas this option simply does not exist. However, more and more foreign tour operators are running treks in parts of the area, and there are many local agents, especially in centres such as Srinagar, who will gladly arrange a trek for you.

Areas

Kashmir: The state of Jammu and Kashmir contains some of the most attractive and popular mountain country in the Himalayas. This includes not only the well-known Kashmir of Dal Lake and Srinagar fame, but also the trans-Himalayan Ladakh and the remote valley of Zanskar. The trekking opportunities are enormous and probably the most accessible and easily-arranged of those in the western Himalayas. One particular attraction of trekking in Kashmir is the masses of flowers almost everywhere, enhanced by the fact that you are there in summer (rather than spring or autumn, as in the monsoon areas).

Srinagar is the main town of the vale of Kashmir, and it is an important starting point for many treks and excursions, with ample facilities, offices and shops. It is connected by road, via high passes, to Ladakh and Leh, and there is relatively easy access to a number of hill stations, ski sites and start points for treks.

South-west of Srinagar, the Pir Panjal range provides some easy, attractive treks. The hill stations like Gulmarg can be reached easily by road and used as bases for short one or two-day trips up into the mountains. Longer treks are limited by military restrictions, though trekking along the range is not too difficult.

East of Srinagar lies the main trekking area, in the Sindh and Lidder valleys. This is an area of beautiful, almost alpine scenery, with good initial access from hill stations like Sonnamarg and Pahalgam, which are themselves easily reached from Srinagar. This area is free from military restrictions, and presents a mass of possibilities to satsify most tastes; there are high passes, glaciers, marvellous scenery and some reasonably high peaks (though by no means the highest of the Himalayas). There are also interesting attractions like the cave at Amarnath, which is the subject of a major Hindu pilgrimage each August around full moon. Around 20,000 pilgrims make the trip each year to see Shiva's ice statue, so you need to decide whether you wish to be involved in this mass movement, and all that it entails, or see the cave at a quieter time.

A little further south, usually beginning by way of Lehinvan (reached by road from Srinagar), it is possible to strike northwards and cross the main Himalayan range over into Ladakh without too much difficulty. The lowest pass which crosses the main Himalayan range here is the Boktol pass, at 4420 m (14,501 ft).

Ladakh, including Zanskar, is part of Kashmir, though very different in character. This is one of the most remote areas in India, and even today access is liable to be difficult via slow and unreliable roads, or by capricious flights to one town only, Leh.

Leh itself is the main town of Ladakh, though it has a population of only some 20,000 people. It provides a good base for trekking in upper Ladakh; however, because it lies so close to the Chinese border, and there is a large military presence there, your only directions lie southwards. The town itself lies at about 3500 m (11,500 ft), so you are quickly into high country, but conversely you have to be sure you are acclimatized at each stage, as it is almost inevitable that you will have to cross a high pass if you go far. The area has remarkable scenery, quite unlike the rest of India, rather like a high altitude desert. It forms the geological boundary between the Himalayas and the Tibetan plateau, and is much more like Tibet than the rest of India. Buddhism is totally dominant, and there are some extraordinary monasteries in extraordinary positions all over the area, such as the tenth-century *gompa* at Lamayuru.

The Zanskar valley, though further south than Leh, is, if anything, even more remote. There is no air access and only partial road access to this isolated part of the world, and until recently it was only accessible over high passes. It is surprisingly populous, but has retained a pure form of Buddhism thanks to its isolation.

There are a number of ways you can trek into the Zanskar valley (or you can get a jeep to Padum in summer), from the north, west or south. From Leh, you can cross the Stok range, then the Zanskar range before reaching the valley. From Lamayuru (the site of the oldest monastery in Ladakh) there is a route which crosses the Zanskar range at the Singi La pass. Alternatively, you can come in from the west, following close to the jeep track, over the Pensi La pass and on down into Padum. You can also walk into the Zanskar valley from the south, without going by road into Jammu and Kashmir at all; this involves continuing by road from Manali, over the Rhotang pass as far as Darcha, and walking from there. The trip involves crossing the main Himalayan range at the high Shingo La (5300m; 17,390 ft), with stupendous views. This southern section is more affected by the monsoon, and has higher snowfall than the northern areas, so a fine balance has to be struck between missing the snow and missing the monsoon. This particular route was the subject of a recent film on British television showing three very different people making the trip; this included an English actress with very little serious walking experience, so it could be considered by any well-prepared walker, though no walk in this area should be undertaken lightly.

Timing: The greater part of this area is free of the worst effects of the monsoon, so its trekking seasons are rather different from those further east. The passes are almost all closed in winter, both to foot and vehicle traffic, and the trekking season is effectively limited, if you are going anywhere high, to June to early October. Some high passes may not open until late June, though few will become closed by the end of October. July and August is the busiest season, though June and September are well worth considering.

Himachal Pradesh: This is the next Indian state eastwards along the Himalayas from Jammu and Kashmir. It includes the colonial town of Simla, British India's former summer capital, and the famous Kulu and Kangra valleys. Again, possibilities for trekking are almost endless, and the land is rather softer and easier than the western parts described so far. As a whole, this area provides an extremely pleasant and easy introduction to Indian Himalayan trekking.

Simla itself is not a particularly good base to start trekking from, because of the proliferation of tracks into the surrounding hills. It is better to start from Kulu or Manali, both of which have reasonable facilities. From Manali, you can trek northwards and westwards up the Solang valley to Beas Kund, and onwards from there if desired. There are superb mountain and glacier views, and lovely campsites, within easy reach of your starting point. Alternatively, you can trek north or north-east, over the Rhotang pass (where the road goes also), or the Hampta pass, into the more arid 'inner valley' area of Lahaul, which is an area much more like Ladakh. If you are planning to spend long in Lahaul, you will need to take ample supplies, as population density is low and food and fuel are scarce. From Manali, there are many other possibilities—east and west along the range, or up various side valleys. As previously mentioned, Manali, or at least the end of the road beyond Manali at Darcha, is also a good starting point for a trek into Zanskar and the extraordinary Phuktal monastery via the Shingo La.

Other good trekking areas in this part of the world include the mountains north of Dharamsala (where the Dalai Lama has his government in exile), from where you can very quickly get into some good country, or you can go over the passes (4000 m; 13,000 ft and up) into the more remote Ravi valley; or the lower Ravi valley, which is accessible directly by road (albeit rather slowly), using Chamba as a base for some further excellent treks into Lahaul or along the Pir Panjal range.

Timing: Himachal Pradesh lies intermediately between the monsoon east and the dry-summer west, and has characteristics of each. The inner valleys of Lahaul and into Zanskar are quite arid and unaffected by the monsoon, though many of the approach routes are monsoonal. In general, the advised seasons for this area are May–June (though the highest passes will be closed until late in this period), or September–October. The combination of monsoon summers, very cold winters, and snow from autumn onwards makes timing more critical than in some areas, with September–October probably being the best bet.

Uttar Pradesh: Uttar Pradesh is an enormous and densely populated state that includes the golden triangle area of Delhi and Agra. It reaches up to the Himalayas for a stretch between Himachal Pradesh and the western border of Nepal and, though not an extensive area, includes much fine Himalayan country. Within its boundaries lie the sources of the Ganges, the most important river in India; Nanda Devi, the second highest mountain in India if you include Kanchenjunga in Sikkim; and the Corbett National Park and Valley of Flowers National Park, with some beautiful mountain country in between. The Himalayas are becoming more simplified here, as we move east, into a narrower range, and the area is somewhat easier to describe than the western areas.

This area is relatively undeveloped as a trekking region, though by no means difficult. There are plenty of possibilities for treks up the valleys from the ends of many roads or tracks. One of the best starting points is at the small town of Joshimath, convenient for treks to Nanda Devi, the Valley of Flowers, and the high peaks and glaciers of the main range to the north-west. There are no military restrictions, so access is very free, except for a current ban on entry into the Nanda Devi Sanctuary, and limitations on movement and camping within the Valley of Flowers National Park area.

Timing: This is quite definitely a monsoon area, though the rainfall is by no means as heavy in summer as further east. Thus the best seasons are May–June and post-monsoon. The monsoon clears fairly early, from late August onwards, and September and October are ideal months for weather and access. If you want to see the displays of flowers in the alpine pastures, for which the area is famous, then you need to go in July or August, braving the wet weather, muddy trails and leeches. A trip in the third or fourth week of August is a good compromise, with a reasonable likelihood of sunshine.

Eastern Indian Himalayas

India stretches northwards to reach the Himalayas again to the east of Nepal, insinuating itself between Bangladesh, Bhutan and Burma. Most of this area is irrelevant at present for the visiting trekker. There is no previous history of foreigners having access to the area. The only section where trekking is permitted is around Darjeeling and within parts of Sikkim, that former kingdom now absorbed into India.

Areas
Sikkim: Sikkim is a tiny mountainous state, covering only just over 7000 sq km (2703 sq miles). It was fully annexed by India in 1975, to become the twenty-second state, and, though now open to visitors, access is still strictly controlled by a permit system. Although internal problems caused by the takeover have largely settled down, it is still considered to be a sensitive border area.

However, with advance planning, or by joining a group, a limited but exciting trek is possible. Although geographically the possibilities are endless and spectacular, in practice you are only allowed at present to trek northwestwards up-country to Dzongri ridge, via Yoksum (Yuksam) and Pemayangtse. This is not a long trek, but it is of superb quality, with wonderful views, particularly of Kanchenjunga, throughout. Once you get going, the area is completely roadless, very peaceful and unspoilt, and more forested than most comparable areas further west. Wildlife is very visible and common, and 110 species of bird were recorded on one occasion, without undue effort, on this short trek in midwinter. Once you get to Dzongri, you can, if your permits are sorted out, spend a few days there, climbing higher in all directions for magnificent views, and you will very probably not see another Westerner. You can return via the beautiful monastery at Tashiding to round off an excellent yet undemanding trip.

Darjeeling lies in West Bengal, though it is close to the Sikkimese border. It is quite definitely Himalayan in character: at an altitude of well over 2000 m (6500 ft), and with excellent views of Kanchenjunga from close by. Treks from Darjeeling are, however, limited both geographically and administratively. Without permits for Sikkim, and with access to east Nepal or Bhutan forbidden, you can only undertake a few short local treks. In the absence of anything else, though, these are well worthwhile and they offer some terrific views. The best treks lie to the north-east, close to the Sikkimese and Nepalese

49. Sherpas at the Mani Rimdu festival, in November. This festival falls in the peak trekking season, and part of it is open to visitors.

borders, reaching as far as Phalut (3600 m; 11,811 ft) or Sandakphu (3636 m; 11,929 ft), offering interesting walking and fine views as far as Everest.

Timing: This far eastern area of the Himalayas is very distinctly monsoon-dominated. Trekking seasons are basically the same as for Nepal, i.e. post-monsoon autumn (October to early December) and spring (April–May). Some trekking is possible into early winter, depending on how high you wish to go, and you can trek in the monsoon if you are prepared to put up with the problems, though no organized groups tend to operate at this time.

NEPAL

Nepal is still the major trekking country in the Himalayas, probably by a very wide margin. There are a number of good reasons for this. It has been open to foreign visitors for at least 30 years, without any significant political or military difficulties during this period, and has built up an enviable reputation as a tolerant, friendly, stable country. Access to the mountains is very easy; quite large planes fly daily into Kathmandu, and good roads connect it to India. Kathmandu itself is not very far from the trekking regions, and reasonable roads connect with starting points or secondary centres. The varied qualities of the Nepalese are well suited to serving the trekking and mountaineering industry, with Sherpas for guides, Thamangs and others for porters, and a variety of races adept at the business side, yet without the greed and dishonesty associated with some races. If you couple this with a plethora of high and famous mountains, from Everest to Annapurna, it is not difficult to see why Nepal is so popular. If you look at any trekking company's brochure, it is Nepal that dominates the routes on offer.

50. Kangtega and Thamserku (right) from Lobuje, just below Everest Base Camp. Khumbu, Nepal.

Having said all that, it should certainly not be claimed that Nepal has all there is to offer in the Himalayas. Each part of the Himalayas is different, and some parts, like the unspoilt wooded mountains of Bhutan, the jagged wild remote peaks of the Karakoram, or the arid deserts of Ladakh, are totally different.

Trekking in Nepal is really very easy, with the exception of a few particularly demanding routes, or if you are trying to break new ground. Group travel is the ultimate in walking luxury, and travelling on your own is made particularly easy—except at very high altitude—by the regularity of inns, lodges and teahouses, and the wide availability of food. For the newcomer to trekking, it is probably the easiest and most welcoming place to start, and there is no shortage of treks to cater for all requirements.

51. Cloud clearing from Ama Dablang, a beautiful peak in the Everest area.

On the other side of the coin—the penalty for becoming too popular, perhaps—are the problems that are occurring along the most used routes. Some treks, particularly in the Annapurna and Everest regions have become distinctly polluted in places by communal toilets and excessive litter, though of course it is only along an extremely narrow corridor. Some of the people along the route have also become distinctly less friendly, with money demanded for photographs, for example, and there is evidence of organized robbery from trekkers in a very few places, though luckily violence is still virtually unknown.

Areas: Nepal has tended to have slightly more clearly defined trek routes than some of the other countries. Whilst there is something of a trend away from this, in an effort to break new ground, it is also true that the classic treks to Everest, Annapurna area, and Langtang still tend to draw the greatest numbers. This is not surprising since, if you are going for the first time, and expect to go only once, you will probably prefer to go on a famous trek to somewhere like Everest rather than risk disappointment on a more obscure trip. Almost anywhere in the Nepalese Himalayas is exciting, though, and you are unlikely to be disappointed wherever you go.

East Nepal: For the purpose of this book, 'East Nepal' means the area west of the Sun Kosi gap, where the Kathmandu-Lhasa road runs through the range.

The best-known trek in this area is still the Lamosangu to Everest trek, and despite its popularity it is still one of the finest. It provides a tremendous introduction to the Himalayas as you trek across the grain of the country, climbing from sub-tropical valleys up to high passes with marvellous views, and then down again, all the way. Eventually, you climb high up into the valleys south of Everest for stupendous views, some fascinating monasteries, a yeti's scalp (!) (see p 76), and some high-altitude glaciers. The normal trek takes you up to Everest Base Camp, or a small peak nearby for better views. If you have time or opportunity, it is worth penetrating some of the less well-known valleys in the area, such as that to the Gokyo lakes and glaciers. Once beyond Namche Bazaar, you are continuously at high altitude, and if flying in or going it alone, you have to be careful to respond to any warning signals of altitude sickness; quite a number of trekkers and mountaineers have died in this area from altitude-related problems.

It can also be possible, with advance planning, to trek on eastwards from here into little-known and dramatic country towards the Arun gorge. There are also alternative routes up into the Everest region from the plains (quicker) or following a higher-altitude route in the Rolwaling Himal (slower and more difficult).

Kanchenjunga lies on the eastern Nepalese border, where it meets Sikkim. It is the world's third highest mountain (8598 m; 28,209 ft), but until very recently has been difficult of access for political reasons. Nepal has now allowed much freer access, and trekking companies are busily developing routes to it. The most likely approach is by air to Biratnagar in south-east Nepal, then by road to Dharan, and on foot thereafter, steadily climbing through the Siwalik hills and the main Himalayan massif. This is wild, unexplored country, and it should be an exciting trek.

Central Nepal: The Himalayas north of Kathmandu and Pokhara provide some of the best and most accessible trekking in Nepal, ranging from easy introductory treks on the lower slopes, to relatively tough trips such as the circuit of Annapurna. One advantage is that very little time is wasted in road trips or walking-in, though on the other hand some of the routes are quite busy.

The Langtang area was one of the first Himalayan National Parks, and its status gives a degree of protection to a fascinatingly varied area, capped by the high peaks of Langtang. Most treks begin from the roadhead at Trisuli, working their way steadily up the main valley towards Tibet, before branching off at Syabru into the Langtang valley. The higher parts of the valley are unspoilt, with striking close mountain views of Langtang, Dorje Lakpa and other peaks, and several glaciers. Beyond Kyangin, you are in remote, completely unpopulated country, and most maps still show the international boundary and valley configuration quite incorrectly here. An interesting way back is via the high Gosainkund lakes (the subject of an annual pilgrimage in August each year), which are deserted and beautiful for most of the year, and out through Helambu to the Kathmandu

valley. You can also branch west from the Trisuli valley into the Ganesh Himal area.

Pokhara, a little further west (only a short plane trip, but quite a long drive from Kathmandu), provides the centre for Annapurna, Dhaulgiri and Kali Gandaki trips. The southern slopes of Annapurna are populous and straightforward, and there are numerous treks providing something for everyone, with wonderful views of the peaks, which are very close to the lowlands here. If you get to Ghorepani, take the opportunity to climb Poon Hill before dawn to experience the incredible sight of the sun rising on Annapurna and Dhaulgiri, with the deepest valley in the world between them!

A rather more demanding, though not especially long trek is up the valley into the 'Annapurna Sanctuary', where you are surrounded by high peaks, including the Annapurnas and Macchapucchare (Fishtail mountain).

52. If trekking in the Annapurna region, or towards the Kali Gandaki, a diversion up Poon Hill to view the dawn over Annapurna and Dhaulgiri is well worth the effort.

The most exciting generally available trek in the area is the circuit of Annapurna, via the Kali Gandaki, Muktinath and Manang, in either direction. This takes you through the Himalayas in the deepest valley in the world, to a quite different land, where rainfall is almost non-existent. You then return via a particularly high pass around the back of the Annapurnas, with some interesting monasteries, a totally different way of life, and the burning-water shrine to keep you interested along the way. Alternatively, you can stop at Muktinath or nearby, and return down the valley, avoiding the high pass, but missing some of the special interest of this trip.

Unfortunately, access to the ancient trans-Himalayan kingdom of Mustang is still restricted for foreigners, though it may one day re-open. The slopes of Dhaulgiri also offer trekking possibilities in magnificent country not visited by organized groups, though this needs some planning.

West Nepal: Nepal west of Dhaulgiri is still virtually a closed book as far as foreign visitors and organized trekking in particular goes. The main problem is access, though the lack of any high peaks or notable sights tends to make it less attractive. There is a national park around Lake Rara, and a trek into this remote area is offered by a few companies, or possible on your own, either by a long walk or a flight first to Jumla. John Pilkington has recently walked right through western Nepal and out into India in winter (with permission), and written of his experiences in the book *Into Thin Air*, for anyone interested in visiting this totally unspoilt part of the world.

Timing: Nepal is entirely monsoon-affected, except for the few trans-Himalayan areas, such as at Muktinath, though of course even these have to be reached through monsoonal regions. The most popular trekking seasons are therefore October–November and April–May. It is, however, markedly further south than the western Himalayas, and some winter trekking is perfectly feasible if you go prepared for cold weather and some snow, and do not expect to cross high passes.

BHUTAN

Bhutan is an independent Himalayan country, separate from, though strongly influenced by, India. Restrictions are more severe than in most other parts of the Himalayas—trekking is

53. Trekkers in Bhutan are rewarded by sights such as the extraordinary 'Tiger's nest' monastery at Taksang, though access is now limited.

permitted, but it is strongly controlled in numbers, routes, and even type of trekker, by the levy of a daily charge. In practice, it is restricted to organized groups, except for special exceptions, and Bhutan trips inevitably tend to cost more than equivalent Nepalese or Indian treks.

It is, however, one of the most exciting places in the world to visit—a real Himalayan Shangri-La. The policy is to only allow tourism or development in such a way that it does not conflict with the country's way of life, and clearly anyone lucky enough to get there benefits from this. It really is totally unspoilt, with an almost unchanged way of life, beautiful buildings, much more forest than the other countries along the range, and masses of wildlife.

Areas: The main treks that are permitted at present are the relatively short treks between Paro and Ha, over the Chili La, and the trek from

54. *The Paro Dzong, and the tower behind, are readily accessible to walkers in Bhutan.*

Paro to Thimpu; a short trek in the Bumthang valley, and a more demanding and longer trek to Chomolhari base camp.

The Chili La trek normally starts at Paro, and you climb quickly through forests to reach the high Kalai La. This is a sacred pass with many prayer flags, and one of the places where the bodies of the dead are placed for disposal by the vultures and ravens—a sensible practice, though one that the Bhutanese government seems embarrassed at Westerners seeing. For several days, you are then on high pastures, with marvellous views of Chomolhari, Kangphu Kang and Kulu Kangri, with more distant views to Kanchenjunga on clear days. Finally, the descent to the drier Paro valley is made. This may be a short trek, but it gives an insight into Bhutan that you cannot get on a tour without trekking.

The trek from Paro to Thimpu is shorter and lower, but gives some good views, a closer look at Bhutanese rural life, and some interesting forests and wildlife.

The trek to Chomolhari base camp is much more demanding and exciting, though by no means exceptionally difficult. It involves crossing four significant passes, and a fair amount of high-altitude work. The trek starts from near Thimpu, reaching base camp in four or five days, and returning via the extraordinary ruined fortress monastery at Drukgyel Dzong to Paro. The middle section of the trek is at continuously high altitude, and the area has a remote, Tibetan feel about it. Blue sheep are often seen here, as well as bears and other large mammals.

Bhumtang, which is further east, is currently visited by specialist natural history tours with organized groups, and it should provide some exciting walking and botanizing.

Timing: Timing for a visit to Bhutan is basically the same as for Nepal, though groups tend not to go trekking in winter, so you are limited to spring and autumn.

TIBET

Trekking opportunities in Tibet are limited and expensive, but they do exist, so they need to be mentioned. Some more adventurous tour operators are now offering Tibetan treks as well as the more long-standing drives through Tibet. The two main possiblities are a trek around Mount Kailash, just north of the India–West Nepal border, or treks around the Mount Everest area from the north of the range.

Mount Kailash is an extraordinary mountain, the subject of considerable religious reverence. It forms the watershed for four main river systems of Asia, and is the hub of the Tibetan plateau. Not surprisingly, it also has many legends and superstitions associated with it. The standard trek offered is to drive from Kathmandu into Tibet, going west along the Tsang-po (Brahmaputra) gorge towards Kailash. The circuit of the mountain involves some high-altitude work and a pass of 5639 m (18,500 ft). It is possible to visit all four of the major river sources.

The Everest region is not easy to get to, and needs special transport. Trekking around the Rongbuk region is permitted, though only organized groups can get permission, and the trip in is a major expedition in itself.

In summary, you can really only expect to get permits and transport for trekking in the Tibetan Himalayas if you go with a group, though it will certainly cost you more than a normal south-side trek. If you especially want to go, you need to check the tour company brochures and book early.

Timing: July and August are the only satisfactory times for high trekking in Tibet, though the route from Kathmandu to Lhasa is open much earlier if this is all you require.

CHAPTER NINE

Outdoor Activities in the Himalayas

In Chapters 7 and 8, the most popular, rewarding and appropriate of possible activities in the Himalayas—i.e. trekking—is covered in reasonable detail. However, there are many other activities, such as skiing, climbing and river-rafting that are becoming increasingly popular. People interested in shooting animals or birds, or in catching fish, will have to look elsewhere for information.

CLIMBING IN THE HIMALAYAS

Climbers have been drawn to the Himalayas since the British occupied India, and the early lightweight expeditions of such legendary figures as Tilman and Shipton in this century drew attention to the marvellous possibilities that the Himalayas offered to the climber. Broadly speaking, serious climbing in the Himalayas, as distinct from trekking and high-altitude scrambling, is an activity open only to relatively few people, though there are some interesting developments that are opening the possibilities more widely.

For a serious climb of any snow peak, permission is generally required, whatever the country, and expeditions need to book the more popular peaks well in advance. Most people intending such a climb will operate within a group expedition, and seek permission, probably through their country's mountaineering council or club. Individual climbs with permission are possible, though the time and red

tape involved may put many people off. At present, for example, Nepal permits climbing only on 76 specified mountains, but expeditions are required to go through a difficult process of obtaining permission, together with the expense of maintaining a mandatory Nepalese liaison officer throughout the expedition. The Indian tourist office publishes a booklet on *Trekking and Mountaineering in the Himalayas*, which details some of the peaks that can be climbed, though they, too, require booking of the peak, a royalty, a liaison officer, and a team of joint Indian-foreign personnel for sensitive areas. Approaches should be made through the Indian Mountaineering Federation in Delhi. Bhutan permits climbs on just one or two peaks, with another being added every two years, though they are anxious that Bhutanese should not be used as guides or porters.

An interesting alternative is now being offered by several trekking/adventure tour companies, allowing you to join a relatively small-scale and straightforward pre-organized climbing expedition. The requirement for joining such groups is money, of course, and a certain standard of fitness and ability, depending upon the peak. Nepal has designated about 20 'trekking peaks', which can be climbed with little more formality than a normal trek, though in most cases the conditions experienced are much more arduous. The highest peaks may be as high as 6600 m (21,650 ft), which offers plenty of serious climbing possibilities for the enthusiast, particularly on snow and ice rather than rock. The additional difficulties produced by the high altitude need to be overcome, and the organized expeditions allow a reasonable amount of acclimatization and training *en route*. It goes without saying that a peak of this height is likely to provide a quite exceptional viewpoint for the adjacent mountains, giving an extra dimension over ordinary trekking, in addition to the satisfaction of achievement. Current prices for such trekking ascents are around £2000 from the UK, which includes flights and most food and equipment for a 28-day trek and climb.

Although the Himalayas provide endless opportunities for more ordinary medium-altitude rock climbing, especially for those wishing to climb away from the masses, it is a long (and expensive) way to go for something that can be obtained at home, and there will almost inevitably be a considerable walk-in on which to carry the equipment. Nevertheless, a bit of rock climbing can provide an extra dimension to a trek for those interested and prepared for it. There is plenty of rock to climb!

SKIING IN THE HIMALAYAS

At present, the only organized skiing areas in the Himalayas lie in north-west India, in several areas between Kashmir and Uttar Pradesh. Some have a reasonably high degree of facilities, such as those in Kashmir, whilst others further west are more basic. All are quiet by European standards, and definitely different, with endless possibilities for the more adventurous.

Gulmarg, in Kashmir, is the country's best-equipped resort, with some of the impersonality of European resorts, and six tows servicing the slopes. Good equipment can be hired, and there are English-speaking instructors available, though apparently skiing stops at eleven a.m. sharp for tea to be served on the slopes! Longer courses are available through the Indian Institute of Skiing and Mountaineering. In addition to the normal downhill runs, there are also endless possibilities for the experienced cross-country skier, and the newly-developed 'heli-skiing'. This involves transport by helicopters (a large one to an intermediate base, and a smaller one from there) to a suitable high point determined according to prevailing conditions, from where one can ski down for up to 2000 m (6500 ft), with up to 4–5 hours of skiing in a day.

Further west, there are skiing facilities in Himachal Pradesh at Narkandar from Simla, or Solang Nala out of Kulu and Manali; while further west still, as the brochure says: 'The skiing does not stop at the border with Uttar Pradesh, but sweeps on regardless. At Auli, in Uttar Pradesh, the surrounding peaks of Nanda Devi (7817 m; 25,646 ft) and Kamet (7756 m; 25,446 ft) provide the perfect backdrop to the lofty deodar forests. They in turn shelter the slopes from the Himalayas' icy blasts.'!

So, skiing in India obviously offers something special and a little different, and you can always take a break and explore India afterwards, at an excellent time of year—the skiing season here is roughly December to March. However, it is to be hoped that skiing does not become so prevalent that it starts to cause the environmental problems that it has in Europe.

WHITEWATER RIVER-RAFTING

An exciting and interesting option on Himalayan trips nowadays involves a river-rafting trip. This consists of 'running' some of the faster-moving Himalayan rivers by means of a tough inflatable rubber raft, carrying 6–8 people at a time. On organized trips there will usually be a leader, a waterproof barrel to keep personal gear dry, and a transport service taking camping and other gear around by road. If rafting for several days, this means that you can arrive at a point where your camp has been erected and find your supper is already being cooked!

Apart from being exciting and exhilarating, white-water rafting takes you into areas that no other transport can reach, and the quieter

moments can provide good views of birds, mammals and local people. If camping, you may end up camping somewhere remote and interesting, though if your gear is being carried by road you are limited to near-road locations. It pays not to take more valuables than necessary with you—last time I went river-rafting the barrel slipped its moorings when we became caught in a whirlpool and all my photographic gear sank to the bottom of a deep, fast-flowing river!

River-rafting opportunities exist in many areas of the Himalayas, although it is easiest to arrange in Kashmir and Nepal. The Nepal operations are generally well-organized and efficient, providing all levels of rafting, including three day-trips ending up close to Chitwan National Park—the lower, calmer sections provide wonderful views of birds here. In Kashmir there are operators providing similar facilities, and the Indus is particularly popular as a destination. In Zanskar, it is possible to raft the Zanskar River for six days, given a good deal of experience, beginning at Padam. Generally, for the difficult trips, it is best to go when the rivers are low—autumn in Kashmir, spring in Nepal— but most companies can advise on this. Many inclusive trekking tours now offer a river-raft trip as part of the 'package', and they are worth considering as something exhilarating and different.

THE DARJEELING TOY TRAIN

Between the hill station of Darjeeling and the lower-lying town of Siliguri lies the famous miniature railway, originally built to carry goods from Darjeeling to the plains and back. Nowadays it offers a marvellous journey for the visitor with time to spare. The whole journey from Siliguri to Darjeeling takes about seven

55. The peaks around Everest are one of the most difficult and challenging areas for climbing in the world, the ultimate goal for experienced climbers.

*56. Whitewater river-rafting on the Trisuli River—
an exciting experience!*

hours, including a stop for food—which is
longer than the bus takes—but it is worth it. For
those with less time, or without the inclination
for a whole journey, a short trip to the station at
Ghoom can be made from Darjeeling, and this
can easily be combined with a walk up the
famous viewpoint on Tiger Hill. If you walk up
to see the dawn over the Himalayas from here,
you can usually get a train back to Darjeeling.

The whole line is something of an engineering
marvel, and there are items of interest all the way
along it. The fare is very reasonable, with a
choice of first or second class.

OTHER ACTIVITIES

Although recreational activities are in their
infancy in the Himalayas, other mountain-
related possibilities exist. These include hang-
gliding and pony-trekking, for which Kashmir is
generally the best area. Ponies can be hired in
Nepal, but they are rare, and the trails are
generally not suited to them, so organized pony-
trekking is infrequent. Other activities such as
golf have no especial bearing on the presence of
mountains, so they are not considered in detail
here, though there are several golf courses
around Srinagar, in remarkable scenery.

CHAPTER TEN

The Photographer in the Himalayas

It is something of a cliche to say that the Himalayas are a photographers' paradise, though it is certainly true. The possibilities for pictures are endless, and it is relatively easy to take good pictures there. Somehow, the variety of potential subjects, from snow-peaks and glaciers, through masses of flowers, to close-ups of Bhotia wedding groups, encourages people to take pictures they would not normally attempt nor perhaps even be interested in.

Nevertheless, a huge amount of film is wasted by people who have the wrong equipment or film, or who have not prepared themselves, and an even larger amount of pictures go untaken by those who have either not brought the camera equipment to cope with them, or have run out of film, or who have not developed the skill of seeing good pictures. It is also true that a lot of potentially good pictures fail to materialize owing to camera faults, overheated films, X-ray machines, accidentally-opened cameras, and many other reasons. So, if you want to return with plenty of good pictures, go prepared.

ADVANCE PREPARATIONS

A large part of the secret of good photography lies in advance preparation and a trip to the Himalayas, especially if you plan to stay long, needs more preparation than most.

Selection of equipment

You may or may not already have all the gear you need. If you can buy things especially for the trip, you can choose carefully with the particular problems in mind. If you already have all the gear you need, it becomes a matter of careful weeding out of unnecessary items. Either way, try to consider, in advance:

1 the main types of pictures you expect to want to take;
2 how much equipment you can carry, bearing in mind any other things you will have to carry, together with exposed and unexposed film;
3 the reliability and quality of your equipment;
4 the use to which you intend to put your pictures.

Looking at these in more detail: it is essential that you consider carefully what you are likely to want to photograph. There is nothing more frustrating, for example, than to go with the intention of photographing wildlife, only to find that your lenses are not up to the job; conversely, it is pointless carrying around large heavy lenses if you really do not have a particular interest in using them. I once spent three weeks walking with an Australian who carried a 500 mm telephoto lens all the way, but only used it once—to photograph the moon! There is a problem, of course, in that you are never exactly sure what you will find (unless you are a regular visitor), so you tend to want to prepare for everything. However, your own interests, plus

57. A shy Rai girl, taken using a tripod and remote release.

guidance from this book and other books, should help to give a reasonable indication of your needs. Several suggested 'outfits' are given later, to cover most eventualities.

The amount you are able to carry, and whether or not you will have anyone to help you carry it, is very important. If you are backpacking, you will inevitably have a considerable weight of other things to carry in addition to your camera equipment, together with all your film, both exposed and unexposed. The weight can mount up considerably, and I would urge you to try out your selected equipment on a full day-trip whilst carrying an appropriately-filled rucksack—you wil probably decide to reduce the weight of something afterwards, but this is better than being unable to carry everything when you get there, or having a consistently miserable time from aching back and leg-joints.

If you are with a group, or are hiring porters yourself, you will, of course, have someone to carry things for you. However, this will not solve all your problems. Although a porter will carry your non-essential items for the day, there is no point in them carrying any camera equipment, because you will not be able to get at it during the day—anything you need to use, you will have to carry, though of course you will be relieved of the need to carry a heavy rucksack. If you are seriously intending to do a lot of photography, or are making a film, then you will need to hire a porter especially for the purpose, and give them a lighter load than normal; porters with full loads will tend to walk at their own pace, and will rarely be there when you need them quickly.

The reliability and quality of your equipment is important. The act of transporting camera equipment out to the Indian sub-continent, followed, perhaps, by a series of bumpy bus rides, numerous dusty days, heavy rain, high and low temperatures, and perhaps weeks of bumping about in a rucksack, tend to expose faults in equipment that you did not know were there. The problem is compounded by the fact that you particularly want the pictures, yet you cannot see the results until after the trip, and you cannot usually do anything about any faults when they do arise.

Clearly not everyone can afford to buy the best-quality professional-style equipment, which is the ideal; reliability and ruggedness undoubtedly costs money, though if your pictures are very important to you, then it is definitely worth

58. An old man, with traditional hat, in Bhutan.

considering a professional camera from Nikon, Canon or Pentax. If you are managing with more ordinary equipment, it is wise to get it checked over and serviced well before you go, and have any faults corrected. After the service, allow yourself time to run a film or two through, to make sure the meter and other parts are correctly adjusted.

If you have neither the time nor the money to have your equipment serviced, then at least make sure you run one or two films through, then carefully check them for faults or inaccurate exposure. It is also worth remembering that main centres like Kathmandu or Srinagar have processing facilities for print films, and you can run a cheap film through the camera and get it rapidly processed just to test it; if returning to such a town in the middle of a trip, it can be very reassuring to check things over, or, alternatively, to discover and rectify any faults.

Finally, *the use to which you intend to put your pictures* is very important. If you intend to take 'snaps' to put in an album to show friends, then it is pointless spending a lot of money, and adding extra weight, buying high-quality equipment. By contrast, if you intend to write and illustrate a book of your experiences, or—often even more demanding—write and illustrate an article for a travel magazine, then you need to be sure that your pictures are of high quality, varied in content, and taken on good film.

This will influence you to take a wider range of lenses, reliable equipment, and probably a range of accessories, including a tripod.

Cameras

If you do not want to carry more than the very minimum, and are only interested in pictures to show views, groups of people, rural activities, etc., then a compact camera, using 35 mm film, will be ideal. If you expect to pay about £120 (new price), you should get a good camera with a high-quality lens.

If you are more serious about taking a range of

Suggested outfits for different purposes

Minimum: A good quality, small compact camera, with or without auto-focusing. A small flashgun, matched to the camera if possible. 8–10 medium-speed films, in rolls of 36.

Average: A good Single Lens Reflex (SLR), with automatic metering (e.g. Pentax ME Super), or an autofocus SLR (e.g. Minolta 7000) with 35–70 mm zoom (or something similar) as standard lens plus a 70–210 mm zoom lens for people, more distant views, some wildlife, etc. Polarizing filter. Flashgun. At least 12 rolls of 36 exposure film.

Advanced: 2 SLR bodies, preferably good-quality reliable ones. Autofocus or manual. 28 mm, 35–70 mm, 70–210 mm zoom, possibly with 300 mm lens, too. Extension tubes for close work; filters to include polarizing and UV. Tripod. At least 20 films (36 exp), of more than one film speed e.g. a mixture of 50 ISO and 100 ISO; or some Kodachrome 64, some Kodachrome 200. One body can be kept for views, etc. and the other, with faster film, for more difficult shots of people, wildlife, etc.

pictures, to include, for example, close-ups of local people, flowers, wildlife, magnified shots of different peaks, etc., then you need a single-lens

59. A flashgun is useful for occasional indoor shots, such as these Tibetan refugees making carpets, singing as they work.

reflex (SLR). These all have the option of interchangeable lenses, so that you can take more than one lens and change it as required. Automatic focusing is quite useful, especially if you want to take lots of pictures of local people, giving you quick unobtrusive accurate focusing.

Lenses

If you buy an SLR, the range of lenses open to you is enormous.

A *wide angle* lens (between 24 mm and 35 mm, for preference) is useful for making the foreground dominate the scene, or for giving a great deal in focus. They are *not* especially useful for panoramic views, since they render all the background details smaller than you hoped, turning mountains into molehills.

Zoom lenses cover a wide range of focal lengths. Modern ones stretch from wide-angle, through standard, well into telephoto. For example, a number of 28–210 mm zooms are available. These are temptingly useful, as they cover all the focal lengths you may need in one lens. Their drawback is that they are quite bulky, so even for wide-angle shots or views you still have to carry quite a sizeable lens on the camera, risking more chance of blurring through camera shake. Personally, I find 35–70 zooms to be excellent as standard lenses, with a good 70–210 mm zoom to cover the telephoto requirements.

60. *Close-ups of village features, such as these attractive wooden beehives, are always worth photographing.*

61. *Harvest time, particularly in autumn, is one of the most rewarding times for the photographer, with endless extra scenes, festivals and features to photograph.*

Telephoto lenses are useful for wildlife, more unobtrusive shots of people, pulling in distant mountains, or giving enlargements of mountain tops, together with interesting 'cameo' pictures, selected from a wider scene. A 70–210 zoom or a 200 mm lens will cover most general telephoto requirements; a 300 mm lens is more specialized, if you have a special interest in birds, wildlife, or other unapproachable subjects. Anything longer than 300 mm is rather bulky for carrying around, unless you are sure you need it. A *teleconverter* is a useful accessory, either as 1.4x or 2x magnification, to increase the focal length of whatever lens you have on. For example, a 200 mm lens plus 1.4x converter gives a 280 mm lens. They are light and small to carry. Make sure you get a good one (7 element, not 4 element).

To take close-ups, you can either take a specialist *macro* lens, or take one or two extension tubes, which fit behind the lens to allow any of your lenses to go closer. Close-up lenses, which screw on the front of lenses, are useful but liable to get dirty or broken, and you may need different ones for different lenses.

Some *filters* are useful in the Himalayas. Ultraviolet or skylight (which is slightly warmer) are useful all-purpose protective filters, and they slightly reduce the blue cast at higher altitudes, though this is not marked. If you keep them on the lens as protection, they do need to be kept very clean, to prevent flare or poorer quality pictures resulting.

The *polarizing filter* is probably the single most useful filter to take; it cuts out polarized light when correctly aligned, though this hardly describes its usefulness. Polarizing filters come in rotating mounts, and you rotate them to find the best effect, viewing this through the viewfinder with an SLR. They are especially useful for enhancing the blue of skies, cutting through haze, reducing glare, and preventing reflections from water. They can really enhance the colours of a picture and improve the colour of sky or the definition of clouds, though they are not always a good thing.

If you use black and white film, an orange filter will be the most useful single filter for most people. Square filters, such as the Cokin system, offer more choice and flexibility, but they are bulkier to carry and slower to use than conventional systems, so they are best avoided unless you are used to them.

Flashguns

An electronic flash is a very useful accessory in a number of situations, such as interiors, active situations in low light, night photography, small moving subjects such as insects, or, for the more experienced, as a fill-in light in natural light photography. The best option is a medium-sized (and medium-powered) unit, dedicated to your camera, and able to make use of the TTL flash metering if the camera has it. It helps to have a lead to use the flash off the camera at times, and this should transmit the TTL metering information if relevant. Spare batteries should be carried if you expect to use the flash much.

Tripods

If you are taking the production of photographs seriously, then taking a tripod becomes quite important. It allows you to get consistently sharper, better-composed pictures, with greater depth of field—for example, your landscapes could have everything in sharp focus from 1–2 metres in front of you right through to infinity. The negative aspects are that you have to carry the tripod with you almost everywhere, and that it takes longer to take pictures, but the results are usually well worth it, and will greatly increase the chances of having pictures published.

Film

Selection of film is a much more personal matter than cameras and lenses, though there are a few useful points to consider.

62. A misty April evening, looking out from the fir forests above Syabru towards Ganesh Himal. A tripod is essential for low-light views.

Film type can be slide (transparency), colour print, or black and white. In general, most people use colour print film, but the proportion using slide film tends to go up in areas like the Himalayas. If you only wish to produce an album or display to show friends, then print film is ideal. If, however, you are likely to give talks or lectures, produce an audio-visual display, or have anything published, then slide film is better; you can also have prints made from any particular slide, if desired. Black and white is a more specialized medium, and few people would take just black and white. Some books and magazines only want b/w, so you may find it worth taking some if you have this aspect in mind.

Film speed is a measure of how sensitive the film is to light. Faster films react more, and therefore allow you to use faster shutter speeds or smaller apertures in a given situation. However, they usually cost more, and are of lower quality, than slower films. If you only have one camera, it is best to take films of around 64–100 ISO, perhaps with one or two faster films for special circumstances. If you have two bodies, you can afford to load one with the slowest film you feel happy with, from ISO 25 to 64 (I usually take Kodachrome 25), and load the other camera with a faster film, from 50–200 ISO. My preference is for a mixture of Kodachrome 25, 64 and 200, though other people prefer Fujichrome or Ektachrome. It is wise not to be tempted into a cheap offer of masses of film that you do not know, or which is out-of-date. Try anything first to make sure you like it. If using print film, there are numerous good print films of around 100–200 ISO, though again you should test it first.

Whatever you take, *make sure you take more than enough film*; you will take more pictures than expected, and it is hard to find *reliable* film on the Indian sub-continent.

Miscellaneous

Make sure you take spare batteries for your camera, if it works on them—there is nothing more aggravating than having your camera become inoperative miles (or days) from anywhere, and there are few stockists of camera batteries anywhere in the Himalayan region. Spare flash batteries are useful, too, and it is best to start out with fresh ones.

Cleaning cloths or tissues, such as those made by Prophot, are essential to keep equipment clean. A notebook and pencil for an *aide-memoire* completes the equipment.

EN ROUTE

Most people fly for at least part of their journey to the Himalayas. If so, you will be faced with the dreaded X-ray machines at all airports. These pose a potential problem to photographers in that X-rays *can* fog film under certain circumstances, possibly ruining it. X-ray machines vary greatly in their ability to affect films, and films themselves vary in their sensitivity—the faster the film, the more liable it is to be fogged. As a general rule, take film with you as hand luggage, and, where possible, ask for it to be hand-searched rather than X-rayed, though this is certainly not always easy to arrange. If you have any fast films, pay particular attention to them.

On the overland parts of the route your greatest problems are likely to be dust, heat and theft, depending upon how and where you are travelling. Try to keep the equipment and film as protected from dust and heat as possible (film ages very quickly in high temperatures), and keep your eye on it at all times. Small unprotected items are the most likely to go astray, while a closed bagful is a little more noticeable, so it is slightly less likely to disappear. Once you get into the hills, away from the populous plains, you are likely to have much less trouble.

63. *'Fish-tail' peak, Nepal, with its shape mimicked by the casually-stacked 'dokos'.*

IN THE HILLS

If you are on a hotel-based tour staying in Kathmandu, Darjeeling, or somewhere similar, your problems, once you arrive, are little different from those of a photographer at home, except that you will probably run out of film more quickly! If you are taking to the hills, on foot, or even by jeep or bus, your organization has to be more specific.

How you carry the camera equipment is important. If you have just a simple camera with no accessories, there is no real difficulty, except for organizing your exposed and unexposed films. If you have more equipment, though, you need some means of storing it with easy access. My own preference is for a waist-mounted Camera Care Systems bag (the 'Alternative workbench'), which allows rapid access to equipment and film, even if you are wearing a rucksack as well. Any large or less regularly-used items can be stored in the rucksack, along with exposed films, and the main supply of unexposed film. Obviously, what you choose will depend on the amount of equipment you have, what else you have to carry, and what you are doing. Shoulder bags can be fine for a few days, but soon give rise to aching shoulders and even knee problems due to walking unevenly.

If you are taking notes about pictures as you go along, in order to identify villages, mountains, or things people have told you along the way, then you need some means of identifying the films later. It is useful to have a spirit-based fine-point pen to write on each as it is completed, or daily in advance if you only take a film or less each day. This can be cross-referenced to the notebook, and transferred to the film return address label when you get home. Keep both exposed and unexposed film as cool as possible, in a safe place. I prefer to keep it all with me in

my rucksack even when I am with porters, just to be sure.

Periodically, you should check the camera over. Examine the shutter, aperture, wind-on, etc., without a film in (but not on a windy day or anywhere dusty). You should also check the film chamber for any dust, and carefully clean it out—dust can get into this section so easily, and it may scratch any number of films without your knowing. If you have two cameras, or a friend with a camera, it is worth periodically comparing meter readings to see that they are remaining accurate, followed by a shutter speed test. *If you change the film speed on one to make them comparable, remember to change it back!*

Opportunities

It is hardly necessary to take space to suggest opportunities for pictures—the problem usually lies in resisting them, rather than finding enough to take. A few suggestions may be helpful, though.

For landscapes and general scenes, it is worth trying to get up early to get pictures with greater impact. Dawn over a range of mountains from a good viewpoint can be really quite spectacular, and it is worth taking several pictures as the light changes. If you are near a lake, the early morning mist and soft light are likely to enhance the pictures. You will also often find that there are fewer people about and there is little wind, so it is generally a good time to be out. Evenings can produce some similar opportunities, and sunsets can be spectacular, though generally dawn is better.

People provide an endless source of picture opportunities in the Himalayas, from wedding groups to facial close-ups. People vary enormously in how much they are prepared to be photographed; in general, the people in the west, who are mainly Muslim, are most reluctant, and should certainly not be pushed. Some hill people are perfectly happy to be photographed, though in some well-used routes in Nepal, many people expect to be paid for the privilege.

64. A simple water-powered flour mill. Thamang village, Nepal.

Wherever you are, it is always worth looking out for close-up or cameo pictures that will enliven any talk or album. The detail on a carved window, an old farm implement, a carved prayer stone, a cobweb with dew on it, etc., will all make interesting pictures. If you have in mind a particular talk or show that you propose to give, it is worth jotting down the range of pictures you want and making sure you remember to take them. It is very easy, for example, to forget to take pictures of your companions, of your house, or the ancient bus that took you to your starting point.

Go well prepared, and you are certain to come back with some interesting pictures to make anyone else green with envy!

CHAPTER ELEVEN

Protecting the Himalayan Environment

The Himalayan environment, with its steep slopes, its primeval forests, its ancient cultures and its rich wildlife, is, without doubt, under threat. Just a few decades ago, many parts of the Himalayas were essentially medieval in their lifestyle and culture, isolated from many of the changes going on in the outside world. Yet today hardly anywhere is unaffected, and many parts have changed beyond recognition.

To investigate the changes and requirements of the Himalayas, it is necessary to separate the effects of change on wildlife and natural habitats from those on the local people, though they are inevitably interrelated. The problem in any discussion on the effect of tourism and development on people, is that no one course of action can be clearly said to be 'the best'; and even if there was one it would probably be impossible to attain.

Is it better, for example, that remote people should be shielded from the effects of development and tourism as far as possible, to ensure that their culture and way of life remains intact? But, suppose they suffer severely from diseases that could be cured, or from regular food shortages that new techniques could overcome? Or, suppose that the majority of the tribe themselves *wanted* to have a road built into their area? The opposite argument might be that every person in a country should have the right to electricity, education, health care, clean water, sewage and so on, as a citizen of that country. This sounds marvellous in principle, but the effects on isolated cultures, the acceleration of the process of homogenization of the country, and side effects on population growth and the environment could all be enormous.

Clearly, there are no easy answers, though there are a few pointers. Local people should have much more say in how they wish to shape their destinies, and how they wish to cope with inevitable outside changes; and development aid should be geared much more towards sustainable small projects, based on local knowledge, that will actually help people be self-sufficient rather than just looking grandiose, spending a lot of money on experts, and encouraging dependence on outside aid.

As an individual, there is relatively little one can do, except by exercising one's vote whenever relevant, and making your views known. As a traveller in the Himalayas, it makes sense to travel with as little ostentation as possible, respecting people's customs, disposing of any litter, etc., as carefully as possible, treating other people as equals (it is surprising how many visitors still treat local people as inferiors), and generally leaving as few traces of your visit as possible.

The natural environment is more straightforward, except that it relates to the livelihood of the people living there, and except for the fact that experts disagree on the scale and solutions to the problem. It *is* generally agreed that there *is* a problem—forests are declining, wildlife everywhere is on the decrease, and populations of people are increasing rapidly.

Mountains are more resistant to change than lowlands in that they cannot be subjected to the mass agriculture industry techniques of flat, fertile areas, but they are also very subject to erosion where their tree cover is removed, and, in any case, they often represent the last wildernesses in otherwise intensively-cultivated and settled areas, which means that we cannot afford to let mountains change too much.

It is true that there is a gradually-expanding chain of national parks and wildlife reserves in most countries along the chain (see p 128), and a gradually increasing awareness of the needs of wildlife and the value of unspoilt areas in tourism. It is easy to be led into thinking that these solve the problem—on their own they do not. Firstly, national parks and reserves may exist in little more than name only, and be subject to the same over-grazing, over-felling

and general over-use as other areas around them; secondly, to be left with a chain of isolated, unspoilt areas, separated by hostile intensively-used, heavily-settled countryside is no solution at all. It greatly increases the tourism pressure on the protected areas (and probably the domestic grazing pressure, too, as all the area around is overused), and in themselves the reserves cannot be large enough to retain the full spectrum of Himalayan wildlife. Apart from the species that never occurred in them in the first place, because of differing requirements, there is also the problem of migratory animals, or animals requiring huge territories, that will not be able to

65. Building yet another high-altitude hotel. The consumption of local materials for building (especially wood), and the subsequent use of resources by visitors, generally exceeds the region's capacity for regeneration.

*66. In the dry season, branches are continuously
collected for fodder, causing gradual deterioration
of the forest environment.*

maintain viable populations in reserves or parks alone. Also, once areas become isolated, they become more vulnerable; for example, a major fire, drought or earthquake in a key reserve could wipe out everything it was intended to pre-serve—and there is nowhere from which the populations can recolonize.

This may paint a bleak picture, but fortuna-tely we are still a long way from this situation, albeit heading towards it. There are more hopeful signs. Aid projects seeking to protect the environment are beginning to incorporate the needs of local people more, making the plans sustainable into the future; in India, strong village movements are arising with the aim of protecting the village environment (mainly the forests), not only against outside logging con-tractors, but also against over-use by the people themselves. It takes a long time for traditions to change in remote villages, and many villagers will just accept the gradually disappearing forests with a shrug rather than change, but nevertheless there *are* changes, and once they have come about, they are unlikely to be reversed. All wildlife conservation has to begin with the conservation of the habitat, so there is a strong link between these village-based conser-vation movements and the conservation of wildlife.

As visitors to this unique area, we should minimize our use of wood, never buy anything that might have involved exploitation of local wildlife, and generally treat the natural environ-ment with great respect. It needs all the help it can get!

VISITING WILDLIFE RESERVES AND NATIONAL PARKS

Although reserves and national parks are by no means the only places where the visitor to the Himalayas can see wildlife, they certainly repre-sent some of the best areas. Generally speaking, there are higher concentrations of animals and birds, and better examples of natural habitat, in such areas; in addition, there may be better facilities, such as hides, and better information aimed at helping you to see what you are interested in. Set against this, though, there may be more restrictions on where you can go, although generally such limits will only be imposed for the protection of the visitor.

The concept of national parks, wildlife reserves, and other protected areas, varies from country to country. Generally speaking, national parks are large areas of exceptional scenery, frequently with a resident human population, that exist to protect the landscape, the way of life, the wildlife and its habitats, and to encour-age access by visitors. Parts may be treated as more intensive nature reserves, and sometimes the whole park is treated as such. Nature reserves, or wildlife reserves, are usually (though not necessarily) smaller, and are more intensi-vely managed and protected with wildlife in mind. Often, there are no resident humans, and all agricultural activities (especially grazing of domestic stock) are prevented if they compete directly with the wildlife. Usually there are better facilities for viewing wildlife than in the more general national parks.

Afghanistan

Afghanistan has, apparently, no named national parks or reserves. For the fortunate visitor, there are a number of interesting areas within the 'Himalayan' mountains of the east part of the country. The Salang Pass, on the main road north from Kabul, gives easy access to some wonderful mountain country, all completely unforested. The Bamian valley is well-known for its Buddhist statues, but it is also of interest as an area of mixed habitat. The incredible lakes of Band-e-amir, accessible by rough tracks to the west, have a very rich flora, together with interesting semi-desert birds and mammals, such as pikas, everywhere. The Hajar valley is a staggeringly impressive Grand-Canyon-like valley, accessible by road, with interesting bird life.

There are also small forested areas in the extreme east of Afghanistan, in Nuristan, though access to here is virtually impossible at present.

Pakistan

There are few official reserves or national parks in the Himalayan section of Pakistan. Most of the higher, wilder areas offer something of interest to the naturalist, and some of the upper valleys are heavily forested, so there are a wide range of species; including both the rich alpine flora and birds and mammals of open hill country, and the flora and fauna of coniferous forests.

The Khunjerab National Park lies high in the northern territories of Pakistan, across the Karakoram highway on its way to China, though there is little to show for its park status to differentiate it, ecologically, from surrounding land. The Khunjerab Pass, at an extraordinary 5275 m (17,306 ft), marks the border with China, so this is a difficult and remote area.

India

India has suffered considerable losses of habitat in recent years, due largely to a rapidly increasing population and improved agricultural techniques. Although such losses still continue, at a government level India has shown great concern for the environment, and many local communities have taken up the challenge to protect their own areas. As a result, the network of national parks and reserves is now extensive, though they vary greatly in size, value and quality of facilities and management.

Kashmir: The **Dachigam** wildlife sanctuary is probably the best-known and most accessible of Kashmir sites, only 22 km (14 miles) from Srinagar. It is a beautiful area, famous for its population of the rare Kashmir stag, or hangul (see p 76), of which it contains the only really viable population left in the world. There are also both black and brown bears, leopards, and a good cross-section of western Himalayan flowers, birds and other wildlife. It is possible to trek and camp in the park, in some beautiful scenery, with a permit from the Chief Wildlife Warden in Srinagar.

Other parks or reserves within the state include: **Kishtwar National Park**, which lies well to the south-east of Srinagar, and covers about 400 sq km (155 sq miles) of mountainous forests and open areas, up to about 4800 m (15,750 ft). There is a rich mixture of wildlife, including both west Himalayan specialities such as hangul and ibex, as well as more widespread species.

There are a number of other reserves or sanctuaries within the Srinagar area, including ones at **Pahalgam** and **Gulmarg**.

High in the barren wastes of Ladakh lies the **Hemis High Altitude National Park**, some 30 km (19 miles) west of Leh. It covers a huge area (*c.* 600 sq km or 232 sq miles) of high altitude plateau and valley, giving protection to some of the specialized flora and fauna of the area, such as snow leopard and blue sheep. Facilities and management are minimal, but access is easy and there is a park office in Leh.

Himachal Pradesh: This area is less well-known and less-visited than Kashmir, and the monsoon influence makes summer visiting more difficult. The **Great Himalayan National Park** protects a huge area of mountainous country near Kulu, with most Himalayan habitats and a wide variety of birds, plants and mammals present. Facilities and information are rather limited, though access is easy.

The **Manali Sanctuary** is only small, but is noted for its richness of mammals and birds. It lies very close to the town of Manali and access is easy.

Uttar Pradesh: This is one of India's largest states, much larger and more populous than the whole of Nepal. It includes several hundred kilometres of the west-central Himalayas, bordering West Nepal.

The **Govind Sanctuary** lies in the mountains

on the Himachal Pradesh border in partly forested country, with good populations of species such as serow, leopard, brown bear and musk deer.

The **Kedarnath Sanctuary** covers a huge area of the Garwhal Himal, with a marvellous range of habitats and much undisturbed temperate forest. It is noted as a musk deer area, though even here these are by no means frequent.

The **Nanda Devi National Park** protects some exceptional scenery and habitat around Nanda Devi, India's second highest mountain (7816 m; 25,643 ft). The flora and fauna are both very rich, though they have undoubtedly declined within the last 50 years. Access is on foot only and there are no residential facilities. At present, access to the park is limited.

The **Valley of Flowers National Park** protects one of the most famous areas of the Himalayas—Frank Smythe's *Valley of Flowers*, so vividly described in his book of the same name. It is an exceptional place, not only for the wonderful displays of flowers in summer, but also for its scenery and general wildlife. Unfortunately, to experience the flowers you also have to experience the monsoon, though a visit in September will catch some flowers in better weather.

Sikkim: Sikkim is India's smallest state, occupying only 7300 sq km (2820 sq miles) in total. It is wholly Himalayan and almost wholly mountainous in character. Despite its small size, it boasts a large and impressive national park, the **Kanchenjunga (Kangchendzonga) National Park**, which occupies about a tenth of the country. It includes some spectacular scenery, around part of the world's third highest mountain, and an exceptional range of habitats. The eastern Himalayas, here, have a very different flora and fauna to the western, and, in particular the flora is much richer with exceptional numbers of primulas, rhododendrons and orchids. There are also populations of clouded leopard, snow leopard, blue sheep, serow, tahr, and many other species. It is best visited out of the monsoon season and is subject to the restrictions applying to any visit to Sikkim – (see p 96).

Nepal

Nepal is a wonderful country for the naturalist to visit, with opportunities to visit an extraordinary range of habitats—from subtropical forest to the highest mountains in the world—all in a very small area. Although its best-known park—**Chitwan**—lies outside the Himalayas, there are several other ones of enormous interest within the Himalayan chain. The furthest west is the **Lake Rara National Park**, established around the catchment area of Nepal's largest natural lake, lying at about 3000 m (9850 ft). The catchment is largely forested with mixed conifers, and there is a reasonable, though not spectacular, range of wildlife to be seen. It is a remote and little-known area, unlikely to be top priority for the first-time visitor to the Himalayas, but with its own special characteristics.

The **Shey Wildlife Reserve** covers some 400 sq km (155 sq miles) of trans-Himalayan habitat in the Dolpo region, more Tibetan in character than Nepalese. The area has good populations of typical high-altitude trans-Himalayan species such as blue sheep, snow leopard, and the elusive wild yak. There are no facilities and access and permits are both difficult.

The **Langtang National Park** is the most accessible of Nepal's mountain parks, lying due north of Kathmandu in an area of beautiful peaks running up to the Chinese border. With an area of 1710 sq km (660 sq miles), it is also the largest of the parks, encompassing an enormous range of scenery and habitat from upper subtropical to the top of Langtang Lirung, at 7245 m (23,700 ft) with many types of forest represented. As a result, a wide range of plants, mammals and birds typical of the central Himalayas occur, though there are few spectacular rarities, and the mammal life is difficult to see.

The **Sagarmatha** (or **Mount Everest**) **National Park** lies in some of the most spectacular scenery in the world, around the highest mountains in the world. There is a fine mixture of high-altitude habitats, with coniferous and temperate deciduous forest, rhododendron scrub, high-level birch and juniper woods, and vast areas of mountain pasture. There are also cultivated areas within the park, often as excluded 'islands'. Bird and mammal life is rich, and it is a good area for seeing many high-altitude south-slope specialities such as choughs, snow pigeon, eagles, blood pheasants, snow-cocks and vultures.

Bhutan

Bhutan is a paradise for naturalists, with a very high proportion of forests left, a rich flora and fauna, and little in the way of hunting or depredation from the relatively small population. Reserves are relatively few, but also relatively unnecessary. The **Jigme Dorji Reserve**, high in the Himalayas, running up to the Tibetan border, is of particular value for its sizeable population of snow leopards and other high-altitude species.

Tibet

Tibetan parts of the Himalayas have a very low population, so they are undisturbed in some ways, but there is ample evidence of increased sheep farming causing decreases in the indigenous mammal populations, and of Chinese soldiers using automatic weapons to kill mammals and birds. There are no formal reserves within the Himalayan area.

Bibliography

There are endless books on the various aspects of the Himalayas, many of which are still in print.

The great majority are available in normal bookshops, though the greatest variety are undoubtedly available in bookshops in the Himalayan area, especially in Kathmandu, Srinagar and Darjeeling.

Some publishers have especially concentrated on the Himalayan or Indian area, and these may be mentioned in summary only (e.g. the Lonely Planet guides).

Ali, Salim. *Field Guide to Birds of the Eastern Himalayas*. Oxford University Press, Bombay, 1977.
    Indian Hill Birds. Oxford University Press, Bombay, 1979.

Bezruschka, Stephen. *A Guide to Trekking in Nepal*. The Mountaineers, Seattle, 1981.

Dor Bahadur Bista. *People of Nepal*. Ratna Pustak Bhandar, Kathmandu, 1980.

Fisher, James F. (ed). *Himalayan Anthropology: the Indo-Tibetan Interface*. Mouton de Gruyter, Berlin, 1979.

Fleming, R., Fleming, R. and Bangdel, J. *Birds of Nepal*. Kathmandu, 1976.

Gibbons, Bob and Ashford, Bob. *The Himalayan Kingdoms*. B.T. Batsford Ltd, London, Hippocrene, New York, 1987.

INSIGHT GUIDES. Apa Productions, Singapore.
    India. 1985.
    Indian Wildlife. 1987.
    Nepal. 1985.

LONELY PLANET GUIDES. Lonely Planet 'Travel Survival Kits', South Yarra (Australia).
    India. 1987, 1990.
    Kashmir and Ladakh. 1985
    Kathmandu and Nepal. 1978.
    Pakistan. 1987.
    Tibet. 1986.
    Trekking in the Indian Himalaya. 1986.
    Trekking in the Nepal Himalaya. 1986.

Hickman, Katie. *Dreams of the Peaceful Dragon*. Gollancz, London, 1988.

Mountfort, G. and Cubitt, G. *Wild India*. Collins, London, 1985.

Nicolson, N. *The Himalayas*. Time Life Books, Amsterdam, 1975.

Olschak, B., Gansser, A., *et al*. *Himalayas*. Facts on File, New York, 1987.

Peissel, M. *Mustang, Lost Tibetan Kingdom*. Collins, London, 1968.

Pilkington, John. *Into Thin Air*. Allen & Unwin, London, 1985.

Polunin, O. and Stainton, A. *Flowers of the Himalayas*. Oxford and Delhi (cheaper in India), 1984.

Prater, S.H. *The Book of Indian Animals*. BNHS, Bombay. 1971.

Pye-Smith, Charlie. *Travels in Nepal*. Aurum Press, London, 1988.

Schaller, G. *Stones of Silence: Journeys in the Himalaya*. Andre Deutsch, London, 1980.

Stacey, Allan. *Visiting Kashmir*. B.T. Batsford Ltd, London, 1988.

Swift, Hugh. *Trekking in Nepal, West Tibet and Bhutan*. Hodder & Stoughton, London, 1989.

Appendix

BEST TIMES FOR VISITING THE HIMALAYAN AREA

Afghanistan	1 May–30 Sept.
Pakistan	1 May–30 Sept.
India:	
Kashmir & Ladakh	1 May–30 Sept.
Himachal Pradesh	20 April–20 June and 10 Sept.–31 Oct.
Uttar Pradesh	15 April–28 June and 25 Aug.–12 Nov.
Sikkim	1 April–31 May and 1 Oct.–31 Dec.
Nepal	5 March–31 May and 1 Oct.–31 Dec.
Bhutan	5 March–31 May and 1 Oct.–15 Dec.
Tibet	15 June–15 Sept.

COMPANIES ARRANGING TREKS AND OTHER TOURS IN THE HIMALAYAS

UK

Chandertal Tours,
Devonshire Cottage, Jevington, Eastbourne, Sussex.
Specialists in NW Indian Regions.

Classic Nepal Ltd.,
33 Metro Avenue, Newton, Derbyshire DE55 5UF. 0733 873497.

Cox and Kings Travel, Ltd.,
St. James Court, 45 Buckingham Gate, London SW1E 6AF. 071-834 7472.
Specialists in Indian and Himalayan tours, including photographic and natural history tours.

Exodus,
9 Weir Rd., Balham, London SW12 0LT. 081-675-5550.
Offer a wide range of treks, climbs and specialist tours to most Himalayan areas.

Explorasia,
FREEPOST, London SW1P 4YZ. 071-630-7102.
Offer a wide range of adventurous and specialist treks throughout the Himalayas.

Hann Overland,
268–270 Vauxhall Bridge Rd., London SW1V 1EJ. 071-834 7337.

High Adventure,
91 Telford Ave, London SW2 4XN. 071-674 8997.
Offer mountaineering and trekking tours.

High Places, ,
15 Spring Hill, Sheffield S10 1ET. 0742 682553.
Offer treks throughout the Himalayas.

Karakoram Experience,
The Trekkers Lodge, 32 Lake Rd., Keswick CA12 5DQ. 07687 72966/72267.
Offer treks throughout the Himalayas.

Naturetrek,
40, The Dean, Alresford, Hants. S24 9AZ. 0962 733051.
Specialists in natural history tours.

Roama Travel,
Lark's Rise, Shroton, Blandford, DT11 8QW. 0258 860298.

Sherpa Expeditions,
131A Heston Rd., Hounslow, Middx. 081-577-2717.
Long-established Nepal and general Himalayan specialists.

Twickers World,
22 Church St, Twickenham, Middx. TW1 3NW. 081-982 7606.
Offer a limited range of Himalayan tours.

Australia

Qantas Adventure Club,
Viva Holidays, 10th Floor, 141 Walker St., N. Sydney, NSW 2060. 02-963 0711.

The names of other tour operators are normally held by the tourist offices of the relevant Himalayan countries. The addresses are:

Government of India Tourist Office,
Carlton Centre, 55 Elizabeth St., Sydney NSW 2000. 02 232 1600;
and: 8 Parliament Court, 1076 Hay St., West Perth WA 6005. 06 321 6932.

Nepalese Consulate:
PO BOX 54, Mosman 2088, Sydney. 02-960-1677.

United States

Government of India Tourist Office,
30 Rockefeller Plaza, 15 N. Mezzanine, New York NY 10020. 212 586 4901.
and: 201, N. Michigan Avenue, Chicago IL 60601. 312 236 6899.
and: 3550, Wilshire Boulevard, Suite 204, Los Angeles. CA 90010. 213 380 8855.

Royal Nepal Embassy,
2131, Leroy Place, Washington DC 20008. 667-4550.

Index

(figures in italics denote illustrations)